Classic

TAPAS

Authentic Spanish recipes

THE ELUSIVE WORLD OF
THE TAPA

Spanish tapas are born of two divinities: wining and dining, yet have inherited neither the history of the former nor the solemnity of the latter. Instead they have established their own personality related, above all, to the refinement of all that is small, to the vivacity of the ephemeral, and to the seduction of the imprecise. Like all that is small and brilliant, the tapa appeared by dint of an almost spontaneous generation, leaving no trace of its history. All gourmets have their own theory about the origin of the tapa, and versions can even be found in encyclopaedias. Some state that tapas came about as a result of innkeepers covering glasses of wine with small pieces of cheese or sausage to stop flies and mosquitoes from falling in (*tapar* means to cover in Spanish), while others say that tapas began to be served at the entrances to inns to satisfy the thirst and hunger of travellers who would halt briefly on their journey but had no time to get down from their horses or carriages even for a bite to eat and a glass of wine. No one has been able to verify these historical origins, and not even their inventors have taken their own creations seriously. Nobody knows and will possibly ever know how tapas came into being, because the recording of origins and histories has only ever been valid for important things and major events, and tapas have always

formed part of a world of miniatures. The only certainty seems to be that tapas originated in Andalusia.

The only essential feature to define a tapa is its smallness, its modest amount. According to the renowned dictionary of the Royal Academy of the Spanish Language, tapas are *"small portions of food served as an accompaniment to a drink in bars, taverns, etc."* The inconsistency of their smallness and their very nature as an accompaniment rob them of their relevance and of any personal identity, and instead place them in an elusive world, brimming with slightness, insinuation, relationships, elegance and unconcern, aspects that take up such an infinite space in the world of refinement. Precisely because of their size, tapas have to be perfect, or as perfect as possible. Their ingredients should be of quality, their preparation painstaking; they should be served at their best and their presentation should be immaculate but simple.

Since their origin tapas have been anything but static, taking shape in every kitchen and typified differently in every tavern, inn and home. Like good songs, tapas roam from one region to another quite naturally, and although they share a common origin they never taste quite the same from one town to another, if the innkeeper or the housewife really take pleasure from their creations. This embodiment means that all varieties of cooking are represented by the plurality of tapas. They symbolise the creativity, skill, ingenuity and zeal of the people that create them.

Anyone who enjoys a tapa from to time usually does so with a certain euphoria, as the charm of the snack generally goes hand in hand with pleasant company. However, the lack of formality in a tapa goes best with a little bit of ceremony, making it an established custom at fixed times for those brief interludes before a proper meal.

A drink and a few tapas with family and friends is a delight and is one of the best ways to make the daily routine more enjoyable. Those who relish a tapa or two understand what life is all about, something that is surely more than a coincidence.

Almost all ancient cities have demonstrated the wisdom of their history, each with its area where tapas are a speciality and from which a notable joie de vivre emanates. These neighbourhoods compete in the number of visitors with the historical areas, full of art and well informed tourists. The apparent contradictions between one area and another are perhaps no more than two interesting aspects of life, and exploring one just as much as the other is the best way to really get to know a town. On returning home, we recall with equal pleasure the historic monuments in a Renaissance square and the preparation and taste of the tapas we have enjoyed. The spheres in which tapa addicts move are a modern conquest,

and tourist guides now pay much closer attention to these areas.

The seduction of the tapa is not merely social; anyone who has succumbed to these tasty morsels in a bar or tavern has also tried to reproduce the pleasure of such titbits at home. As well as more formal meals, we also feel like a 'nibble' at home with our family or friends. The charm lies to a certain extent in becoming the protagonists of an intimate, social activity.

You don't have to be a professional cook to prepare delicious, varied and ingenious tapas, and serve them at just the right time. And with these easy to prepare dishes, tapas can end up being a meal in themselves.

The recipes in this book have been written for modern living, for the men and women of today who take an increasing interest in the personality of their homes. The recipes included here cover all the regions of Spain. With such variety and experience, these are tapas that will find a place in any kitchen and in any home.

Rafael de Haro

ALCACHOFAS CON JAMÓN
ARTICHOKES WITH HAM

Ingredients

- 6 artichokes
- 200 g (7 oz) cured ham (*jamón serrano*)
- 1 onion
- 1 hardboiled egg
- 1 tin peas
- 1 lemon
- Olive oil
- Salt

Preparation

Remove the stems and tough leaves from the artichokes. Heat plenty of water with salt and the juice of a lemon (to prevent them from browning) in a pan. Add the artichokes when the water begins to boil and cook until they are tender and can be easily pierced with a larding needle. This should take about half an hour. Remove from the water and put to one side.

Chop an onion and gently sauté in oil. Dice the ham and add to the pan when the onion begins to brown. Stir well and add the artichokes and peas. Add a small amount of water from the tin of peas and simmer for a couple of minutes.

Serve hot, garnished with slices of hardboiled egg.

ALCACHOFAS RELLENAS DE CARNE

ARTICHOKES STUFFED WITH MINCE

Ingredients

- 6 artichokes
- 1 lemon
- 1 large onion
- 3 tomatoes
- 300 g (10 oz) minced beef
- 2 cloves garlic
- Parsley
- 1 egg
- 3 slices creamy cheese
- Olive oil
- Salt

Preparation

Remove the stems and tough leaves from the artichokes, and hollow out the centres to form small bowls. Place a small cut in the base so they stand upright. Cook in plenty of salted boiling water, with lemon juice to prevent them from browning. Cook for around half an hour, until tender. Drain and put to one side.

Chop an onion and gently fry in oil. Peel and chop the tomatoes and add to the onion when it begins to brown. Season and strain through a colander.

Cover the bottom of an ovenproof dish with half of the sauce and place the artichokes on top.

Meanwhile, crush salt, garlic and parsley in a mortar and mix in with the meat before browning with a little oil. Beat an egg and mix with the mince once it is done, together with the rest of the tomato sauce.

Use this mixture to stuff the artichokes, and cover them with half a slice of cheese. Place in the oven and grill until the cheese has melted.

Serve straight away.

ASADILLO DE PIMIENTOS
ROAST PEPPER SALAD

Ingredients

- 4 red bell peppers
  (*pimiento morrón*)
- 2 tomatoes
- 3 cloves garlic
- Olive oil
- Salt
- Vinegar

Preparation

Preheat the oven at a medium temperature and roast the peppers, tomatoes and garlic, all in the same dish and drizzled with olive oil. After 20 minutes or once all the vegetables are roasted, place the peppers in a deep dish, cover with a cloth and leave for a few minutes to sweat (this makes them easier to peel). Once peeled, remove the seeds and slice into strips.

Peel the tomatoes and blend in a food processor with the garlic and a pinch of salt. Pour into a jug and add the juices left from the baking tray, together with five tablespoonfuls of olive oil and a dash of vinegar. Spread this mixture over the peppers.

Serve at room temperature.

BERENJENAS CON QUESO
AUBERGINES WITH CHEESE

Ingredients

- 2 aubergines
- Flour
- 200 g (7 oz) creamy cheese
- 2 eggs
- Milk
- Nutmeg
- Olive oil
- Salt

Preparation

Peel the aubergines and chop into 1 cm (1/2 in) slices. Sprinkle with salt and leave to sweat for 30 minutes, then dry with a cloth. Coat in flour and fry in hot oil until golden brown.

Line the bottom of an ovenproof dish with a layer of aubergine, then place a layer of cheese on top, complete with a second layer of aubergine.

Beat the eggs, add a little milk and a pinch of nutmeg; pour over the aubergines and place the dish in a preheated oven at a medium temperature until the egg sets.

Serve hot.

BERENJENAS GRATINADAS
AUBERGINES AU GRATIN

Ingredients

- 2 aubergines
- 150 g (5 oz) cured ham (*jamón serrano*)
- 150 g (5 oz) creamy cheese
- Tomato sauce
- Oregano
- Olive oil
- Salt

Preparation

Wash the aubergines and, without peeling, chop lengthways into thick slices. Sprinkle with salt and leave for half an hour to sweat. Dry with a cloth and fry on both sides with a little olive oil until tender.

Lay the slices on an oven tray, placing a little tomato sauce, a slice of ham and another slice of cheese on top. Sprinkle with oregano and grill until the cheese melts.

Serve piping hot.

BROCHETAS DE VERDURAS
VEGETABLE BROCHETTES

Ingredients

- 150 g (5 oz) mushrooms
- 1 aubergine
- 1 courgette
- 1 red pepper
- 12 cherry tomatoes
- Olive oil
- Vinegar
- Pepper
- Basil
- Salt

Preparation

Wash the courgette and aubergine and chop into 3 cm (1 in) cubes. Clean the mushrooms with a damp cloth and cut in half, or in quarters if large.

Chop the pepper in the same way as the aubergine and courgette. Wash and dry the tomatoes.

Place the vegetables on skewers, alternating ingredients and placing a piece of pepper between each one.

Sprinkle with salt, freshly ground pepper and basil. Drizzle with oil and a few drops of vinegar.

Place in a preheated oven at a medium temperature, or under the grill, for 15 minutes.

Serve hot.

CALABACINES RELLENOS
STUFFED COURGETTES

Ingredients

- 3 courgettes
- 500 g (1 lb) minced pork
- 1 onion
- 2 cloves garlic
- 1 handful spring garlic (ajetes)
- 200 g (7 oz) wild mushrooms
- 2 carrots
- 4 eggs
- 1 tin foiegras
- Béchamel
- Grated cheese
- Olive oil
- Salt

Preparation

Slice the courgettes lengthways; if they are very large slice each half in two. Remove the flesh and put to one side.

Cook the courgettes in a pan with salted boiling water for five minutes, drain well and put to one side.

Crush the garlic in a mortar, mix with the mince and leave to marinate for an hour. Meanwhile, finely chop the onion, ajetes and carrot, and fry in a little olive oil.

When the vegetables are soft, add the meat and a pinch of salt, stir well and add the sliced mushrooms. After a few minutes add the flesh from the courgettes and cook on a low heat for ten minutes. Beat the eggs and add together with the tin of foie gras, and mix thoroughly.

Stuff the courgettes with this mixture and place in an ovenproof dish. Prepare a béchamel and cover each courgette with the sauce. Sprinkle with grated cheese and grill.

Serve hot.

CEBOLLAS RELLENAS
STUFFED ONIONS

Ingredients

- 8 medium onions
- 2 tins bonito or tuna
- 1 tin red bell peppers (*pimiento morrón*)
- 1 hardboiled egg
- Tomato sauce
- White wine
- Parsley
- Garlic
- Olive oil
- Salt

Preparation

For the filling: flake the tuna and add to the finely chopped hardboiled egg, pepper (together with part of the juices) and two tablespoonfuls of tomato. Mix well.

Peel and the onions and hollow them out with a corer. The walls should be thin, but not so thin that they split. Stuff the onions with the filling and cover the hole with the first ball removed from each onion.

Fry the onions in hot oil, splashing them with a skimmer until they brown. Place them in a casserole dish and put to one side.

For the sauce: chop the onion left over from the core and fry in olive oil. Crush two cloves of garlic and a few sprigs of parsley in a mortar together with half a glass of white wine and add to the frying pan when the onions begin to brown. Add a little tomato sauce. Bring to the boil and pour over the onions. Season and leave to cook on a low heat for an hour and a half.

Strain the sauce before serving.

CHAMPIÑONES CON JAMÓN
MUSHROOMS WITH HAM

Ingredients

- 350 g (11 oz) mushrooms
- 100 g (4 oz) ham
- 1 onion
- 1 small green pepper
- 2 cloves garlic
- 1 tomato
- Olive oil
- Salt
- Parsley
- Chilli pepper

Preparation

Clean the mushrooms (if they are not too dirty, wiping them with a damp cloth is sufficient) and cut into slices.

Finely chop the onion, garlic and pepper, and fry in a little olive oil. When they begin to brown, add the chopped parsley and the peeled and chopped tomato, and cook for a further five minutes. After this time, add the diced ham and a touch of chilli (to taste); fry gently, and add the mushrooms. Continue frying for a few minutes, stirring well, until the mushrooms are slightly tender. Check for salt if necessary (remember that the ham will add salt of its own).

Leave to stand for a few minutes and serve while hot.

CHAMPIÑONES RELLENOS
STUFFED MUSHROOMS

Ingredients

- 16 large mushrooms
- 2 onions
- 1 small red pepper
- Parsley
- 3 cloves garlic
- 250 g (8 oz) chorizo sausage
- Black pepper
- Olive oil
- Salt

Preparation

If the mushrooms are not too dirty, they are best cleaned by wiping them with a cloth, but if they contain a lot of earth they should be washed in water and then dried quickly. Remove the stalks and chop them finely. Leave the caps whole and put them to one side.

Finely chop the onion and pepper, and heat olive oil in a frying pan, adding first the onion and then the pepper. When they brown, add the chopped mushroom stalks and leave to cook until most of the liquid sweated out has evaporated.

Remove and discard the skin of the chorizo, and chop into pieces. Stir into the vegetables, together with the crushed garlic. Fry on a low heat for eight minutes.

Meanwhile, wash and finely chop the parsley. Season the chorizo mix with salt and pepper, bearing in mind that the chorizo is already quite salty. Add the parsley and stir well.

Finally, stuff each mushroom cap with a small amount of this mixture and place in an ovenproof dish. Place in a preheated oven for ten minutes until the mushrooms begin to brown.

Serve piping hot.

EMPAREDADOS DE CALABACÍN
COURGETTE 'SANDWICH'

Preparation

Wash and dry the courgettes and cut into slices about 1/2 cm (1/4 in) thick. Sprinkle with salt and place in a colander for the courgette to sweat.

Meanwhile, cut the cheese and ham into slices the same size as the courgette (use the rim of a class or cup). Slice the tomatoes to the same size.

Once the courgette has sweated, rinse and dry with a clean cloth or kitchen roll. On top of each courgette slice place a slice of cheese, a slice of ham and a slice of tomato, and cover with a second slice of courgette to form small sandwiches. Coat in flour, dip in beaten egg, and finally roll in breadcrumbs.

Heat olive oil in a pan and fry until golden brown.

Serve hot.

Ideal served with a light sauce on the side.

Ingredients

- 2 large courgettes
- 150 g (5 oz) cooked ham
- 150 g (5 oz) creamy cheese
- 3 tomatoes
- 2 eggs
- Flour
- Breadcrumbs
- Olive oil
- Salt

ENDIBIAS AL QUESO DE CABRALES
ENDIVES WITH CABRALES CHEESE

Ingredients

- 3 endives
- 150 g (5 oz) Cabrales cheese (or any other strong blue cheese)
- Milk
- Single cream
- 1 lemon
- Ground pepper
- Salt

Preparation

Discard the outer leaves of the endives, wash the rest under the tap and dry with a cloth, making sure the leaves do not break.

Place a frying pan on the heat and add the cheese, together with a small glass of cream and another of milk. Check for salt. Add the juice of half the lemon and stir well to form a light cream. Strain through a colander and leave to cool.

Place the endives on a plate and pour over the hot sauce just before serving. Sprinkle with freshly ground pepper.

ESPÁRRAGOS RELLENOS DE SALMÓN
ASPARAGUS STUFFED WITH SALMON

Ingredients

- 6 thick white asparagus
- 150 g (5 oz) smoked salmon
- 1 egg
- Flour
- Olive oil
- Salt

Preparation

Peel the asparagus from the tip down. Bring a pan of salted water to the boil, add the asparagus and cook for around 35 minutes. Use a larding needle to check if they are done. Remove from the water and place on a cloth to dry. Tinned asparagus can also be used.

Open the asparagus up lengthways like a hotdog. Fill with strips of salmon, coat in flour and dip in egg. Fry in hot oil.

Serve at once. Can be accompanied with a simple lettuce and tomato salad.

ESPÁRRAGOS VERDES CON JAMÓN
GREEN ASPARAGUS WITH HAM

Ingredients

- 10 green asparagus
- 3 slices cooked ham
- Butter
- Flour
- Milk
- Grated cheese
- Salt

Preparation

Remove and discard the hard parts from the asparagus. Place in boiling salted water for 10 to 12 minutes (depending on the thickness). After this time, use a larding needle to check they are tender, then remove from the pan and allow to drain.

Wrap each asparagus in a slice of ham, but do not cover the tips. Place on a baking tray.

Meanwhile, prepare a béchamel sauce: melt a tablespoonful of butter in a pan, add a tablespoonful of flour and slowly stir in milk. Season and leave to cook for 5 minutes. Pour the sauce over the asparagus, leaving the tips. Sprinkle with grated cheese and place under the grill until golden brown.

Serve straight away.

MOUSSE DE ESPÁRRAGOS
ASPARAGUS MOUSSE

Ingredients

- 1 tin white asparagus
- 1 onion
- 1/4 l (8 fl oz/1 cup) single cream
- 4 eggs
- Butter
- Pepper
- Salt

Preparation

Chop the onion and sauté in a frying pan with a tablespoonful of butter. When the onion becomes transparent, add the asparagus together with part of their juice. Leave to boil for two minutes and then blend in a food processor.

Beat the eggs in a large bowl and add the cream. Season with salt and pepper and then add the asparagus mix, stirring well. Pour into a metal pudding mould.

Heat the mould in a bain marie until the mousse sets.

Allow to cool before removing from the mould.

Serve cold with mayonnaise on the side.

PATATAS ALIOLI
ALIOLI POTATOES

Ingredients

- 500 g (1 lb) potatoes
- 1 egg
- 1 lemon
- 3 cloves garlic
- Olive oil
- Parsley
- Salt

Preparation

Peel, wash and chop the potatoes. Cook in a pan with salted water until soft and can be pierced easily with a skewer. Once cooked, remove from the pan, drain and place in a bowl.

While the potatoes are cooking, prepare the alioli. Make a mayonnaise with one egg, olive oil, the juice of half a lemon, salt and two tablespoonfuls of tepid water (for a more liquid mayonnaise).

In a mortar, crush three cloves of garlic to form a smooth paste and add to the mayonnaise bit by bit, mixing well.

Spoon the alioli over the potatoes and sprinkle with chopped parsley.

Serve chilled.

PATATAS BRAVAS
SPICY POTATOES

Ingredients

- 500 g (1 lb) potatoes
- 3 tomatoes
- Tabasco sauce
- Olive oil
- Salt

Preparation

Wash the potatoes, without peeling, and boil in plenty of salted water. Once cooked, drain, peel and chop the potatoes into evenly sized cubes.

Fry the potatoes in very hot oil until they begin to brown, then remove and place on a platter.

Meanwhile, chop the tomatoes and fry in a small pan with two table-spoonfuls of olive oil. Strain this sauce through a sieve and mix with a tea-spoonful of Tabasco to taste.

Spoon the sauce over the potatoes.

Can be served hot or cold.

PATATAS DE LA TÍA CARMEN
AUNT CARMEN'S POTATOES

Ingredients

- 750 g (1¹/₂ lb) potatoes
- 3 cloves garlic
- 100 g (4 oz) cured ham
  (*jamón serrano*)
- Butter
- Flour
- Milk
- Grated cheese
- Olive oil
- Salt

Preparation

Peel the potatoes and rinse well. Cut into slices (not too thick), sprinkle with salt and fry in plenty of hot oil. When they are half done, add the garlic cut into thin slices and fry until the potatoes are golden brown. Remove from the oil and place in an ovenproof dish.

Cut the ham into strips and sauté in the same pan before placing over the potatoes.

Meanwhile, prepare a béchamel sauce: melt 2 tablespoonfuls of butter in a pan and add 4 tablespoonfuls of flour. Stir well and add milk bit by bit, stirring constantly for 5 minutes. Season with salt and pour over the potatoes. Sprinkle with grated cheese and grill until the cheese is golden brown.

Serve straight away.

PATATAS RELLENAS
STUFFED POTATOES

Ingredients

- 8 medium potatoes
- 50 g (2 oz) cured ham *(jamón serrano)*, diced
- 150 g (5 oz) minced beef
- 100 g (4 oz) wild mushrooms
- 2 onions
- 1 clove garlic
- Parsley
- Saffron
- White pepper
- Meat stock
- White wine
- Olive oil
- Salt

Preparation

Peel and wash the potatoes. Use a corer to hollow them out, leaving a thin wall but ensuring that they do not split.

Finely chop an onion and fry in a little olive oil. Clean and chop the mushrooms and add to the pan when the onions begin to brown. When the liquid from the mushrooms evaporates, add the ham, mince and chopped parsley. Season with salt and pepper and leave to cook for five minutes.

Use this mix to stuff the potatoes.

Fry the potatoes in plenty of hot oil until they are brown all over, remove and place in a casserole dish. Gently fry the potato pieces left over from the core and use them to line the bottom of the casserole. Strain part of the oil used to fry the potatoes and prepare the following sauce: sauté a finely chopped onion, crush the garlic and parsley in a mortar together with a glass of white wine, and add to the pan. Bring to the boil and add a glass of stock and the roasted saffron. Add this sauce to the potatoes and cook on a low heat until tender.

Serve hot.

PIMIENTOS RELLENOS DE BACALAO
RED PEPPERS STUFFED WITH COD

Ingredients

- 10 *piquillo* red peppers (fresh or tinned)
- 150 g (5 oz) salt cod (preferably flaked)
- 1 large onion
- 1 green pepper
- Tomato sauce
- Flour
- Butter
- Milk
- Olive oil
- Salt
- Black pepper

Preparation

Desalt the cod by soaking in water 24 hours before use.

Heat a little olive oil in a frying pan and poach half the onion and the green pepper, both finely chopped. When they are lightly browned, add the cod (well rinsed and flaked) and fry for a few minutes.

Meanwhile, prepare a light béchamel sauce with the flour, butter and milk, and add to the cod. Check for salt. Use this mix to stuff the peppers and place them in an ovenproof dish.

For the sauce: heat a little olive oil in a frying pan and poach the other half of the onion; before it browns add tomato sauce and ground black pepper (to taste); leave to boil for a moment, then strain and pour over the peppers.

Finally, place in the oven for 5 to 6 minutes at a medium heat.

Serve hot.

PIMIENTOS RELLENOS DE CHIPIRONES
RED PEPPERS STUFFED WITH CUTTLEFISH

Ingredients

- 12 *piquillo* red peppers (fresh or tinned)
- 500 g (1 lb) cuttlefish
- 2 onions
- 2 cloves garlic
- 1 green pepper
- White wine
- Olive oil
- Salt
- Squid ink

Preparation

Clean and chop the cuttlefish.

Finely chop the onion, garlic and green pepper and gently fry in olive oil. Add the cuttlefish before the vegetables begin to brown, together with a dash of white wine. Cook for 20 minutes, adding the squid ink and checking for salt half way through.

Remove the cuttlefish from the sauce, stuff the peppers and place them on a baking tray, pouring the sauce over the top.

Place in the oven for 5 to 6 minutes on a medium heat.

Serve hot.

PIMIENTOS VERDES RELLENOS DE CARNE
GREEN PEPPERS STUFFED WITH MINCE

Ingredients

- 6 round green peppers
- 500 g (1 lb) beef mince
- 1 large onion
- 2 carrots
- 1 glass white wine
- Meat stock
- 1 egg
- Stale bread soaked in milk
- Flour
- Olive oil
- Pepper
- Salt

Preparation

Cut away the top of the peppers with a knife and take care to remove all the seeds.

Finely chop half an onion and a carrot and fry in olive oil until the onion browns. Season the mince, add to the pan and cook until done. Soak the breadcrumbs in milk, rinse well, and add to the mixture together with a glass of white wine. Leave to cook for five minutes, then remove from the heat, beat an egg and add to the pan, stirring well.

Use this mixture to stuff the peppers, and place in an ovenproof dish.

To prepare the sauce, finely chop the other half of the onion and the remaining carrot and fry until they begin to brown, then add a tablespoonful of flour, a generous drop of white wine and a cup of stock, and leave to cook for a few minutes. Strain the sauce through a sieve or muslin and pour over the peppers. Place in the oven at a medium-high heat for around 45 minutes, until the peppers peel. Spoon the sauce over the peppers several times while they cook to make sure they do not dry out.

Serve hot.

PISTO CASTELLANO
CASTILIAN RATATOUILLE

Ingredients

- 3 tomatoes
- 2 onions
- 3 cloves garlic
- 2 green peppers
- 1 courgette
- 1 aubergine
- Parsley
- Olive oil
- Salt

Preparation

Wash the aubergine and chop into 2 cm (3/4 in) cubes. To remove the bitterness, season with salt once chopped and leave for fifteen minutes. Rinse off any water sweated out and dry with absorbent kitchen paper. Top and tail the courgette and dice, as with the aubergine. Slice the pepper into strips and the onion into rings, and chop the garlic.

In a casserole with hot olive oil, fry the onion until transparent, and add the pepper and garlic. Then add the aubergine and courgette and fry for around seven minutes.

Meanwhile, in a pan with boiling water, scald the tomatoes for two or three minutes to remove the skin. Peel the tomatoes, remove the seeds and any hard parts, and dice. Add to the ratatouille, check for salt and leave to cook on a low heat for fifteen minutes, until almost all the liquid has evaporated. Sprinkle with chopped parsley before removing from the heat.

Serve hot or at room temperature.

PISTO CON GAMBAS
RATATOUILLE WITH PRAWNS

Ingredients

- 10 fresh prawns
- 2 tomatoes
- 2 green peppers
- 2 onions
- 100 g (4 oz) ham
- Meat stock
- 2 eggs
- 2 cloves garlic
- Olive oil
- Salt

Preparation

Place the tomatoes in a pan with boiling water for a few minutes, then remove and leave to cool before peeling and removing the seeds. Chop and put to one side.

Meanwhile, dice the pepper, chop the onion and slice the garlic.

Heat olive oil in a casserole and fry the onions until transparent, then add the pepper and garlic and fry for a further seven or eight minutes. Dice the ham and add to the mixture, followed by the tomato. Stir well and add the prawns and a small cup of stock. Season with salt and leave to cook for five minutes. Remove the prawns from the dish, then pour the mixture over the eggs (previously beaten), stirring continuously. The ratatouille should have a fairly liquid consistency.

Serve hot in a bowl or platter with the prawns placed on top.

PUDIN DE VERDURAS
VEGETABLE PUDDING

Ingredients

- ½ cabbage
- 2 carrots
- 2 spring leeks
- 1 red pepper
- 2 onions
- 3 cloves garlic
- 4 tomatoes
- 100 g (4 oz) cured ham (*jamón serrano*)
- Stale bread
- Milk
- 3 eggs
- Butter
- Breadcrumbs
- Olive oil
- Salt

Preparation

Wash the vegetables. Chop the cabbage, carrots, leeks and red pepper in julienne and cook in salted water for around 20 minutes until tender. Remove from the heat and drain.

Fry the onion and garlic in olive oil. Peel and chop the tomatoes, and add to the pan when the onion begins to brown. Season and leave to cook for 10 minutes.

Put half this sauce to one side, and add the vegetables to the other half. Mix well and add the stale bread, previously soaked in milk, the chopped ham, previously sautéed in a little oil, and the beaten eggs. Pour into a mould (greased with butter) and sprinkle with breadcrumbs.

Place the mould in a bain marie for 30 minutes.

Strain the other half of the sauce and spoon over the pudding before serving.

PUERROS GRATINADOS
LEEKS AU GRATIN

Ingredients

- 4 leeks
- 4 slices cooked ham
- 4 slices cheese
- Grated cheese
- Flour
- Butter
- Salt

Preparation

Top and tail the leeks, removing all the green stalks, and wash well. Cook in salted water for 15 minutes. Remove the leeks and put the cooking water to one side.

Wrap each leek in a slice of cheese, and then a slice of ham. Place in an ovenproof dish.

Meanwhile, prepare a béchamel sauce: melt two tablespoonfuls of butter in a saucepan. Add 3 tablespoonfuls of flour and, stirring constantly with a wooden spoon, slowly pour in the cooking water, making sure no lumps are formed. Cook for 5 minutes.

Pour the sauce over the leeks, sprinkle with grated cheese and grill to brown the cheese lightly.

Serve piping hot.

REVUELTO DE SETAS
SCRAMBLED EGGS WITH WILD MUSHROOMS

Ingredients

- 500 g (1 lb) wild mushrooms
- 6 eggs
- 20 shoots spring garlic (*ajetes*)
- 2 cloves garlic
- White pepper
- Single cream
- Brandy
- Olive oil
- Salt

Preparation

Clean the mushrooms with a cloth and chop into small squares. Marinate for half an hour in a little brandy.

Chop the *ajetes* and slice the garlic cloves and sauté gently in oil for 3 minutes, stirring constantly. Add the mushrooms and cook for a further 10 minutes. Season with salt and pepper.

Light beat the eggs, together with half a cup of single cream, and pour over the mushrooms, stirring well until the egg sets slightly.

Serve hot, sprinkled with chopped parsley.

TOMATES RELLENOS DE BACALAO
TOMATOES STUFFED WITH COD

Ingredients

- 8 medium tomatoes
- 300 g (10 oz) salt cod
- 1 onion
- Butter
- Flour
- Grated cheese
- Olive oil
- Milk
- Salt

Preparation

Soak the cod in water for 24 to 48 hours (depending on the thickness of the fish) to remove the salt, changing the water several times.

Place the cod in a pan with plenty of cold water and bring to the boil. Remove from the heat, cover and put to one side for ten minutes. After this time, drain the cod, remove the skin and bones and flake the flesh.

Meanwhile, wash the tomatoes and slice off the tops. Remove the seeds and part of the flesh. Season with salt and place upside down to drain.

Chop the onion and poach in a frying pan with a little oil. Meanwhile, prepare a béchamel sauce: melt the butter in a saucepan and add the flour, stirring well with a wooden spoon. Slowly pour in the milk. Season and leave to cook until ready. Add the onion and cod and mix well.

Stuff the tomatoes with the sauce and sprinkle with grated cheese.

Grease an ovenproof dish with oil. Add the tomatoes and place in the oven at a medium temperature for 40 minutes, until the tomatoes soften.

TOMATES RELLENOS DE CARNE
TOMATOES STUFFED WITH MINCE

Ingredients

- 8 medium tomatoes
- 200 g (7 oz) minced beef
- 150 g (5 oz) minced pork
- 1 clove garlic
- 1 onion
- 100 g (4 oz) mushrooms
- Pepper
- 1 egg
- Parsley
- Olive oil
- Salt

Preparation

Wash the tomatoes and slice off the tops. Remove the seeds and part of the flesh. Season the tomatoes with salt and place upside down to drain.

Chop the onion and garlic and sauté in a frying pan with a little oil. Season the mince, clean and chop the mushrooms, and add both to the pan. Cook for a few minutes and remove from the heat.

Beat an egg and pour over the meat, together with a teaspoonful of chopped parsley. Mix well and use to stuff the tomatoes.

Grease an ovenproof dish with oil. Add the tomatoes and place in the oven at a medium heat for 40 minutes, until the tomatoes soften.

TOSTAS DE CHAMPIÑONES
MUSHROOM TOASTS

Ingredients

- 4 rounds white sliced bread
- 300 g (10 oz) mushrooms
- 4 eggs
- Single cream
- 3 cloves garlic
- Pepper
- Parsley
- Olive oil
- Salt

Preparation

Clean the mushrooms with a cloth and chop into slices.

Chop the garlic and fry in a little oil, adding the mushrooms before the garlic has a chance to brown. Sauté until all the water has evaporated. Season with salt and pepper.

Meanwhile, beat the eggs, add half a cup of single cream and a tablespoonful of parsley, and pour into the pan, stirring well until the egg sets.

Remove the crusts from the bread (cut into rectangles if preferred) and toast.

Place the mushrooms on top of the toast and sprinkle with parsley.

HUEVOS A LA FLAMENCA
FLAMENCO EGGS

Ingredients

- 100 g (4 oz) peas
- 100 g (4 oz) green beans
- 2 tomatoes
- 1 onion
- 2 cloves garlic
- 100 g (4 oz) chorizo sausage
- 100 g (4 oz) cured ham (*jamón serrano*)
- 1 tin asparagus tips
- Paprika
- 6 eggs
- Olive oil
- Salt

Preparation

Cook the peas and the beans in salted water until tender. Drain and put to one side.

Finely chop the onion and garlic and fry in oil. Scald the tomatoes to remove the skin and chop into pieces. Add to the pan when the onion begins to brown, together with a teaspoonful of paprika. Cook on a low heat for 5 minutes, add the diced ham and cook for another 5 minutes. Add the peas and beans, the chorizo chopped into slices and a small amount of water from cooking the vegetables. Season with salt and leave to cook for a further 5 minutes.

Dive the mixture into individual ovenproof dishes, removing the chorizo first.

Break an egg into the centre of each dish, placing a slice of chorizo and an asparagus tip next to the yolk.

Place in the oven at a medium temperature until the egg white sets.

Remove from the oven and serve straight away.

HUEVOS A LA MARINERA
EGGS WITH TUNA AND ANCHOVIES

Ingredients

- 6 eggs
- 1 tin tuna
- 2 tins anchovies
- 6 stuffed olives
- Lettuce

For the mayonnaise:
- 2 eggs
- Vinegar or lemon
- Olive oil
- Salt

Preparation

Place the eggs in a saucepan with plenty of cold water and a pinch of salt. Bring to the boil and simmer for 12 minutes, stirring occasionally to make sure the yolk stays in the centre. Remove from the water, leave to cool and remove the shells.

Meanwhile, prepare a mayonnaise: place the two eggs in a bowl, together with a tablespoonful of vinegar or lemon juice and a pinch of salt. For a lighter sauce, add a few drops of water. Take a hand blender, place in the bowl and begin to add the oil, moving the blender up and down, until the mayonnaise is ready. Check for salt and lemon.

Cut the eggs lengthways and remove the yolks. Mix four of the yolks with the tuna (drain off the oil) and the mayonnaise. Stuff the egg whites with the mix and place upside down on a platter. Cover with mayonnaise. Place a string of anchovy fillets around each egg, top with half an olive, and finally sprinkle with the two remaining egg yolks.

Decorate the platter with finely chopped lettuce.

HUEVOS RELLENOS DE ALMENDRA
EGGS STUFFED WITH ALMOND

Ingredients

- 6 eggs
- 150 g (5 oz) ground almonds
- 2 tomatoes

For the mayonnaise:
- 2 eggs
- Vinegar or lemon
- Olive oil
- Salt

Preparation

Place the eggs in a saucepan with plenty of cold water and a pinch of salt. Bring to the boil and simmer for 12 minutes, stirring occasionally to make sure the yolk stays in the centre. Remove from the water, leave to cool and remove the shells.

While the eggs are cooking, prepare the mayonnaise: place 2 eggs, the juice of half a lemon or a tablespoonful of vinegar and a pinch of salt in the jug of a hand blender. Add a few drops of water to make the sauce lighter. Begin to pour in the oil, using the blender to obtain the required consistency. Check for salt.

Cut the eggs lengthways and remove the yolk. Mix four yolks with the ground almonds and mayonnaise. Stir well and use to stuff the half egg white. Place upside down on a platter, on a bed of tomato slices.

Serve covered in mayonnaise and with grated egg yolk sprinkled on top.

PINCHO DE HUEVO DURO
HARDBOILED EGG SNACK

Ingredients

- Slices of bread
- Slices of cured ham (*jamón serrano*)
- Smoked salmon
- Eggs
- Prawns
- Mayonnaise
- Olive oil
- Salt

Preparation

Fry the bread in hot oil, remove from the pan and drain on kitchen paper.

Cook the prawns for a minute or two in boiling water with salt. Remove and place in cold water to cool, before peeling and removing the heads.

Meanwhile, cook the eggs in a pan of cold water with a pinch of salt for 12 minutes, counting from when it starts to boil. Once cooked, place in a bowl of cold water to cool and remove the shells.

On each piece of fried bread, place a slice of ham, a slice of salmon and a slice of hardboiled egg; cover with mayonnaise and top with a prawn.

Sprinkle with grated hardboiled egg and serve.

TORTILLA DE CEBOLLA
ONION OMELETTE

Ingredients

- 6 eggs
- 200 g (7 oz) pork loin
- 3 onions
- Olive oil
- Salt

Preparation

Chop the onion and fry gently in a little olive oil, stirring well to prevent the onion from browning.

Chop the pork into small cubes and fry in a separate pan.

Beat the eggs in a bowl and add the onion, the pork and a pinch of salt, stirring well.

Heat a frying pan with olive oil and cook the omelette on both sides.

Serve hot.

TORTILLA RELLENA
STUFFED OMELETTE

Ingredients

- 500 g (1 lb) potatoes
- 6 eggs
- 1 onion
- 2 tomatoes
- 1 tin tuna
- 10 crab sticks
- Lettuce
- 2 hardboiled eggs
- Mayonnaise
- Olive oil
- Salt

Preparation

Peel and wash the potatoes and chop into small cubes. Chop the onion to a similar size. Mix together and season.

Fry the onions and potatoes in plenty of hot oil on a low heat. When they are tender, but before they begin to brown, remove from the pan and shake off any surplus oil.

In a bowl, beat the eggs and season with salt. Add the potatoes.

Pour half of the mix into a frying pan with a little hot oil and allow the omelette to brown, shaking the pan gently to prevent it from sticking. Use a flat plate to turn the omelette over and brown the other side, then remove from the pan and leave to cool. Use the other half of the mix to make a second omelette in the same way.

While the two omelettes are cooling, prepare the filling: finely chop the crab sticks and the hardboiled eggs, and flake the tuna. Bind with mayonnaise.

Place a layer of lettuce leaves on one of the omelettes, followed by a layer of the mayonnaise mix and a final layer of thinly sliced tomato. Cover with the second omelette.

Serve sliced into bite-sized portions.

TORTILLA PAISANA
OMELETTE COUNTRY STYLE

Ingredients

- 500 g (1 lb) potatoes
- 6 eggs
- 100 g (4 oz) green beans
- 100 g (4 oz) peas
- 50 g (2 oz) ham
- 50 g (2 oz) chorizo sausage
- 1 onion
- Olive oil
- Salt

Preparation

Peel the potatoes and chop into small pieces. Finely chop half the onion in the same way.

Heat plenty of olive oil in a frying pan and add the potatoes and onion, together with a dash of salt. Fry on a low heat, stirring occasionally, making sure that they are cooked through, but do not brown.

Chop the beans and cook, together with the peas, until tender.

Chop the other half of the onion and add to a second frying pan with olive oil. Fry until the onion becomes transparent, then add the ham and chorizo (both diced), the beans and peas, and finally add to the potatoes, draining off any surplus oil.

Beat the eggs with a little salt in a deep bowl, and add the mixture to the egg, stirring well.

Heat a frying pan, well greased with oil, and cook the omelette on both sides.

Serve sliced into small portions.

ALBÓNDIGAS DE CARNE
MEATBALLS

Ingredients

- 500 g (1 lb) minced beef
- 150 g (5 oz) minced pork
- 3 cloves garlic
- 3 tomatoes
- 1 onion
- Parsley
- 1 egg
- White wine
- Stale bread
- Pepper
- Flour
- Raisins (seedless)
- Olive oil
- Salt

Preparation

Crush a clove of garlic and a few sprigs of parsley in a mortar, together with a dash of white wine. Place the mince in a large bowl and add the garlic. Mix well and leave to stand for 15 minutes.

Soak the bread in milk and add to the bowl, together with an egg (beat first), salt and pepper. Knead until all the ingredients are mixed together, then make balls and roll in flour. Fry in plenty of hot oil until golden brown, then shake off any oil and place in a casserole.

Strain part of the oil used to fry the meatballs to prepare the following sauce: chop the onion and two cloves of garlic and sauté in a frying pan. When they begin to brown, add the chopped tomato. Cook for five minutes and add a glass of white wine. Boil for three more minutes, then strain the sauce over the meatballs. Add a few raisins and cook on a low heat for 25 minutes. Add a little water to the sauce if it becomes too thick.

Serve hot.

BROCHETAS DE LOMO CON BACON
PORK AND BACON BROCHETTES

Ingredients

- 500 g (1 lb) pork loin
- 250 g (8 oz) bacon
- 350 g (11 oz) mushrooms
- 1 pepper
- 12 prunes (pitted)
- 1 lemon
- Oregano
- Pepper
- Olive oil
- Thyme
- Salt

Preparation

Cut the pork into even-sized cubes and leave to marinate for at least two hours in a container with four tablespoonfuls of olive oil, the juice of half a lemon, thyme, oregano, salt and pepper.

Cut the bacon and pepper into squares. Clean the mushrooms with a damp cloth and leave whole, unless large.

Remove the meat from the marinade and form the brochettes, alternating the pork, pepper, bacon, mushrooms and prunes.

Oven-roast or grill the brochettes for 10 to 15 minutes, turning occasionally and basting from time to time with the marinade juices.

Serve hot.

CALLOS
TRIPE

Ingredients

- 1 kg (2 lb) tripe
- 1 beef shank
- 2 pig's trotters
- 1 calf snout
- 2 onions
- 3 cloves garlic
- Parsley, bay leaf
- Chilli pepper
- White vine
- 150 g (5 oz) cured ham (jamón serrano)
- 100 g (4 oz) chorizo sausage
- Paprika
- Vinegar, Salt
- Olive oil

Preparation

Wash the tripe in plenty of cold water, and leave for an hour in water with salt and vinegar, then rinse until the vinegar smell disappears. Cut into even-sized pieces and boil in a pan for seven minutes. Drain and place in cold water, together with a clove of garlic, a chopped onion, parsley, bay leaf and salt for four hours. Drain and put to one side.

Flame the beef shank, the pig's trotters and the snout, in order to remove any hairs. Scrub with a brush and rinse. Simmer for three hours, then remove from the pan and put the resulting gelatine stock to one side.

Chop the shank, trotters and snout, and mix with the cooked tripe.

Chop the onion and chilli and fry. When the onion begins to brown, add the ham and the diced chorizo. Sauté and add a tablespoonful of paprika.

In a separate pan, fry two cloves of garlic and a few sprigs of parsley, crush in a mortar and add to the onion. Pour in a glass of white wine and leave to boil. Place the tripe, shank, trotters and snout in a casserole dish and pour the sauce over the top. Add some of the gelatine stock (enough to ensure a liquid sauce), season with salt and cook on a low heat for another hour.

Serve hot.

CODORNICES ESTOFADAS
STEWED QUAILS

Ingredients

- 4 quails
- 1 onion
- 3 cloves garlic
- Brandy
- Parsley
- Thyme
- Chicken stock
  (fresh or stock cube)
- Olive oil
- Salt

Preparation

Drizzle the quails with brandy and leave to stand for at least half an hour.

After this time, season with salt and sauté in hot oil until brown, then remove from the pan. Chop the onion, garlic and parsley and fry in the same oil used for the birds. Add the quails again and pour in a touch of brandy and half a glass of stock.

Cook for 20 minutes on a low heat, then strain the sauce through a colander.

Ideal served with small round slow-fried potatoes.

CONEJO A LA CAZADORA
HUNTSMAN'S RABBIT

Ingredients

- 1 rabbit
- 1 onion
- 3 cloves garlic
- Parsley
- Thyme
- 250 g (8 oz) mushrooms
- White wine
- Brandy
- Olive oil
- Pepper
- Salt

Preparation

Clean the rabbit and cut into pieces. Smear with slices of garlic and chopped parsley and thyme. Leave to stand for two hours.

After this time, remove any garlic pieces, season the meat with salt and fry in a casserole dish with hot oil until the pieces are golden brown. Chop the onion and add to the rabbit, together with the garlic. Cook gently until the onion and garlic brown slightly.

Meanwhile, clean the mushrooms with a cloth, chop and add to the rabbit.

Pour in a glass of white wine and half a glass of brandy. Check for salt and pepper.

Cook gently, stirring from time to time, until tender. Add a little meat stock or water if it becomes dry.

COSTILLAS DE CERDO CON PEPINILLOS
PORK RIBS WITH GHERKINS

Ingredients

- 400 g (13 oz) pork ribs
- Pork lard
- 1 onion
- 2 cloves garlic
- Flour
- Vinegar
- 6 vinegar gherkins
- Pepper
- Salt

Preparation

Season the ribs with salt and pepper and fry with a little lard until they brown. Remove from the frying pan and put to one side.

Chop the onion and garlic and fry in the same lard until they are lightly browned. Add a tablespoonful of flour and stir well. Slice the gherkins and add to the pan, together with half a glass of water and a squirt of vinegar. Season and boil for a couple of minutes.

Add the ribs to the pan, and cook until the sauce begins to thicken.

Serve hot.

CRIADILLAS REBOZADAS
BATTERED CALF FRIES

Ingredients

- 500 g (1 lb) calf fries (testicles)
- 1 lemon
- 1 egg
- Flour
- Breadcrumbs
- Pepper
- Olive oil
- Salt

Preparation

Clean the fries with plenty of cold water to get rid of the blood. Remove and discard the surrounding skin, drizzle with lemon juice and leave to stand for an hour.

Place in a metal sieve or colander and scald in a pan of boiling water for half a minute, then remove and dry.

Slice the fries into fillets and season with salt and pepper. Coat the fries in flour, then dip in egg and finally roll in breadcrumbs.

Fry in hot oil until they brown.

Serve straight away.

CHULETITAS DE CORDERO ABRIGADAS
LAMB CHOPS IN BÉCHAMEL BATTER

Ingredients

- 12 lamb chops
- 2 cloves garlic
- Butter
- Flour
- Milk
- 1 egg
- Breadcrumbs
- Thyme
- Olive oil
- Salt

Preparation

Crush the garlic in a mortar, smear over the chops and leave to stand for an hour. Wipe off the garlic with a cloth and season the lamb with salt and thyme. Fry in hot oil, then remove from the pan and put to one side.

Prepare a béchamel sauce: melt two tablespoonfuls of butter in a pan, add four tablespoonfuls of flour, stirring continuously, and slowly pour in the milk. Add salt and cook for five minutes until the sauce thickens.

Take the chops and dip in the béchamel, making sure they are completely covered in sauce. Leave to cool.

Once they are cold, dip them first in egg and then coat in breadcrumbs. Fry in hot oil until golden brown.

Serve hot.

CHULETITAS DE CORDERO CON ALCAPARRAS
LAMB CHOPS WITH CAPERS

Ingredients

- 12 lamb chops
- Onion
- 1 egg
- 1 hardboiled egg
- Tomato sauce
- White wine
- Capers
- Pickled gherkins
- Flour
- Breadcrumbs
- Parsley
- Pepper
- Olive oil
- Salt

Preparation

Season each chop with salt and pepper, then coat in flour, dip in egg and roll in breadcrumbs. Fry in hot oil until golden brown. Remove from the pan, put to one side and strain the oil.

Chop half an onion and fry in the oil used for the chops. When it is cooked add a drop of white wine, two tablespoonfuls of tomato sauce, 15 capers and 2 small gherkins, finely chopped. Season with salt and pepper and sprinkle with chopped parsley. Leave to cook for 15 minutes.

Arrange the chops around the edge of a platter and spoon the sauce into the centre, together with the chopped hardboiled egg.

Serve hot.

ESCALOPINES AL QUESO DE CABRALES
BEEF FILLETS WITH CABRALES CHEESE

Ingredients

- 6 beef fillets
  (small and thin)
- 100 g (4 oz) Cabrales
  cheese (or any strong
  blue cheese)
- Single cream
- Brandy
- Butter
- 1 egg
- Flour
- Olive oil
- Breadcrumbs
- Salt

Preparation

For the sauce: melt two tablespoonfuls of butter and the cheese in a frying pan. Add a glass of single cream and a squirt of brandy. Reduce for three minutes. Blend in a food processor until the sauce is creamy.

Sprinkle the fillets with salt and roll in flour, dip in egg and coat in breadcrumbs. Fry in hot oil and place on a platter.

Serve with the sauce piping hot.

FLAMENQUINES
ROLLED FRITTERS

Ingredients

- 6 thin beef fillets
- 3 eggs
- 6 slices cured ham (*jamón serrano*)
- 36 pitted olives
- 1 onion
- 2 cloves garlic
- Red bell pepper (*pimiento morrón*)
- White wine
- Olive oil
- Salt

Preparation

Stretch out the fillets and season lightly, bearing in mind that the ham will add salt of its own.

Beat the eggs with a pinch of salt and prepare a flat French omelette.

On each fillet place a slice of ham, a few strips of omelette and pepper and a few pieces of chopped olive. Roll up the fillets carefully, making sure that the other ingredients stay in place, and tie the rolls with string or fasten with toothpicks. Fry in hot oil and place in a cake tin.

Finely chop an onion and crush the garlic in a mortar, and fry in the same oil used for the rolls. Add a glass of white wine when the onion begins to brown. Bring to the boil, pour over the *flamenquines* and cook for an hour until the meat is tender (prick to test).

The sauce can be served as it is or strained through a colander.

HÍGADO ENCEBOLLADO
LIVER IN ONIONS

Ingredients

- 750 g (1¹/₂ lb) calf livers
- 2 onions
- 3 cloves garlic
- Parsley
- Bay leaf
- Paprika
- Olive oil
- Salt

Preparation

Remove and discard the film around the liver and cut into small pieces. Season with garlic crushed in a mortar.

Finely chop the onion and parsley and fry on a low heat with the garlic and a small bay leaf. When the onion is tender, season the liver with salt and add to the mixture, together with a tablespoonful of paprika. Turn up the heat and fry for five more minutes.

Serve piping hot, with chips or white rice.

LOMO DE CERDO MECHADO
PORK LOIN WITH BACON STRIPS

Ingredients

- 750 g (1½ lb) pork loin (whole)
- 100 g (4 oz) bacon
- 2 cloves garlic
- Pepper
- Thyme
- Olive oil
- Salt

Preparation

Crush the garlic in a mortar and smear over the meat. Leave to stand for at least an hour.

Meanwhile, slice the bacon into strips 1 cm (½ in) wide.

Once the meat is ready, use a cloth to clean off the garlic and insert the bacon lengthways into the meat, keeping the strips close together.

Season with salt and thyme, and place in an ovenproof dish.

Pre-heat the oven to a medium temperature. Pour a glass of very hot oil over the meat and place in the oven to roast for 30-40 minutes, turning occasionally to make sure it is brown over. Pour a little water over the meat if necessary.

Serve hot in thin slices with the cooking juices spooned over, or cold with mayonnaise.

LOMO DE CERDO RELLENO
STUFFED PORK LOIN

Ingredients

- 750 g (1½ lb) pork loin (whole)
- 100 g (4 oz) minced beef
- 100 g (4 oz) minced pork
- 100 g (4 oz) chopped cured ham (*jamón serrano*)
- 50 g (2 oz) olives
- 50 g (2 oz) red bell pepper (*pimiento morrón*)
- 1 hardboiled egg
- 1 egg
- Brandy
- Thyme
- Olive oil
- Salt

Preparation

Make two cuts lengthways in the pork, without reaching the ends. Put to one side.

Mix the mince and ham together. Finely chop the pepper, the olives and the hardboiled egg, and add to the meat.

In a bowl, beat an egg and mix in all the ingredients, together with half a glass of brandy. Add salt, bearing in mind that the ham and olives are salty ingredients.

Insert the filling in the cuts made in the meat, and tie up with string (not too tight, so that the stuffing is not squeezed out).

Sprinkle the meat with salt and drizzle with hot oil before placing in a pre-heated oven at a medium temperature.

Roast for 40 minutes, basting the meat frequently with its own juices, or with a little water if it becomes too dry.

Leave to cool before untying the string.

Serve hot in thin slices with the cooking juices spooned over, or cold with mayonnaise.

MANITAS DE CERDO ESTOFADAS
STEWED PIG'S TROTTERS

Ingredients

- 4 pig's trotters
- 2 onions
- 1 clove garlic
- Paprika
- White wine
- Black peppercorns
- Bay leaf
- Chilli pepper
- Parsley
- Olive oil
- Salt

Preparation

Use front trotters, as they have more meat. Most butchers sell them ready cleaned and split in two. Tie them with string so they keep their shape during the cooking.

In a pan with plenty of salted water, cook the trotters together with a piece of onion, a clove of garlic, a bay leaf and a few peppercorns. Simmer on a low heat for 3 hours, then remove the trotters from the pan and put the stock to one side.

Finely chop an onion and gently sauté in a casserole dish with a little oil. Crush the garlic and parsley in a mortar, mix with half a glass of white wine, and add to the onion when it begins to brown. Add a teaspoonful of paprika and a bay leaf, and then add the trotters. Cover and cook for an hour, adding stock if the sauce becomes too dry. Add a chilli pepper for a spicier flavour.

Serve hot.

MOLLEJAS AL JEREZ
SWEETBREADS IN SHERRY

Ingredients

- 500 g (1 lb) veal sweetbreads
- 1 onion
- 1 carrot
- 200 g (7 oz) mushrooms
- 1 clove garlic
- Parsley
- Dry sherry
- White pepper
- Olive oil
- Salt

Preparation

Soak the sweetbreads in several changes of water to remove all the blood. Cook in plenty of salted water for 10 minutes. Remove from the pan, leave to cool and remove the skin and suet. Cut into regular-sized pieces.

Finely chop the onion and carrot and sauté in hot oil. When they brown, add the sweetbreads and fry for a few minutes. Clean and chop the mushrooms, crush the garlic and parsley in a mortar with a glass of sherry, and add to the pan. Season with salt and pepper and cook for 20 minutes. Add water if the sauce becomes too dry.

Serve hot.

PASTEL DE CARNE
MEAT LOAF

Ingredients

- 250 g (8 oz) minced chicken
- 250 g (8 oz) minced pork
- 250 g (8 oz) minced beef
- 1 sachet cream of mushroom soup
- 150 g (5 oz) pitted olives
- 3 eggs
- 1 tin foie gras
- Dry sherry
- Pepper
- Butter

Preparation

Using a fork, mix the different minces with the chopped olives, the sachet of cream of mushroom, the beaten eggs, foie gras and a glass of sherry. Season with pepper. No salt is necessary, due to the packet soup mix.

Grease a sheet of tinfoil with butter and place the mixture on the foil in the form of a bow. Wrap this bow up in the foil to keep in all the juices.

Place in the oven at a medium-high temperature for 30 minutes.

Can be served cold with mayonnaise, or hot with mushrooms.

PECHUGA DE POLLO AL JEREZ
BREAST OF CHICKEN WITH SHERRY

Ingredients

- 500 g (1 lb) chicken breast
- 2 cloves garlic
- 1 glass dry sherry
- Chicken stock
- Pepper-stuffed olives
- Flour
- Olive oil
- Black pepper
- Thyme
- Salt

Preparation

Dice the chicken (first removing any skin and bone), season with salt and coat in flour.

Fry the meat in hot olive oil until golden brown, then remove from the pan and season with freshly ground black pepper and thyme.

Heat a tablespoonful of olive oil in a casserole dish and add a glass of sherry and another of chicken stock.

Meanwhile, crush the garlic in a mortar and add to the casserole. Reduce the stock by half, add the chicken pieces, and leave to cook on a low heat for eight minutes.

Finally, chop the olives into slices and add to the chicken.

Serve hot.

POLLO AL AJILLO CAMPERO
CHICKEN IN GARLIC

Ingredients

- 1 chicken
- 6 cloves garlic
- Olive oil
- Brandy
- Salt

Preparation

Burn off the remains of any feathers, wash the chicken, dry well and cut into small pieces.

Thinly slice the garlic and use to rub the chicken pieces, together with a little brandy. Leave to stand for an hour, then remove the garlic pieces and put to one side.

Season the chicken and fry in batches in hot oil until golden brown.

Use part of the same oil to fry the garlic left over from marinating the meat, and pour over the chicken.

Serve straight away, sprinkled with chopped parsley (optional).

POLLO EN ENSALADA
CHICKEN SALAD

Ingredients

- 1 chicken breast
- 1 green pepper
- 1 tomato
- 1 onion
- Parsley
- 2 hardboiled eggs
- Olive oil
- Vinegar
- Butter
- Garlic
- Brandy
- Salt

Preparation

Smear the chicken breast with crushed garlic and leave to marinate for half an hour. After this time, use a cloth to remove the garlic, smear the chicken with butter, and place in an ovenproof dish.

Bring three tablespoonfuls of olive oil to boil in a frying pan, and pour over the chicken. Place in a preheated oven on a medium heat. When the meat begins to brown, baste with a glass of brandy and spoon the juices over the chicken from time to time until the meat is tender. Remove from the oven and leave to cool.

Meanwhile, prepare a vinaigrette dressing: mix a glass of olive oil, vinegar and a pinch of salt in a deep bowl and whisk until creamy. Finely chop the onion, parsley and hardboiled eggs and add to the bowl.

When the chicken has cooled, chop into pieces and arrange on a platter, together with the diced pepper and tomato.

Pour the dressing over the salad and serve.

POLLO EN PEPITORIA
CHICKEN FRICASSEE

Ingredients

- 1 chicken
- 50 g (2 oz) almonds
- 1 onion
- 2 cloves garlic
- 1 egg yolk
- Saffron
- Chicken stock
- White wine
- Olive oil
- Salt

Preparation

Clean the chicken and coat in flames to burn off any feathers. Cut into pieces and season.

In a frying pan with hot oil, brown the chicken evenly all over, then place the pieces in a casserole dish.

Chop the onion and garlic and sauté in the same oil. Toast the saffron and add to the pan, together with a glass of stock and half a glass of wine. Bring to the boil, simmer and pour over the chicken. Cover and cook on a low heat for around half an hour, until the meat is tender.

Crush the raw, peeled almonds in a mortar, together with the hardboiled egg yolk. Mix with a little water and add to the casserole. Cook for a few minutes until the sauce is well mixed in.

Serve hot.

RIÑONES AL JEREZ
KIDNEYS IN SHERRY

Ingredients

- 500 g (1 lb) kidneys (pig or calf)
- 1 onion
- 2 cloves garlic
- Flour
- Parsley
- Dry sherry
- Lemon or vinegar
- Olive oil
- Salt

Preparation

Clean the kidneys, cut into slices and remove any skin and fat. Sprinkle with lemon juice or vinegar and put to one side for half an hour.

Place the kidneys in a sieve or metal colander and scald by lowering into a pan with boiling water for half a minute. Remove and leave to dry.

Crush the garlic in a mortar, add half a glass of sherry and use the mixture to rub the kidneys. Leave to stand for an hour and a half.

Finely chop the onion and a few sprigs of parsley and fry in hot oil. Add the kidneys when the onion begins to brown. Season and cook on a high heat for 5 minutes. Add another half glass of sherry and a tablespoonful of flour. Stir well and cook on a low heat for a further 5 minutes.

Serve piping hot.

RIÑONES SALTEADOS
SAUTÉED KIDNEYS

Ingredients

- 500 g (1 lb) kidneys (pig or calf)
- 1 onion
- 2 cloves garlic
- Parsley
- 20 g (1 oz) pine kernels
- 1 tomato
- 1 hardboiled egg
- Paprika
- White wine
- Vinegar or lemon
- Olive oil
- Salt

Preparation

Clean the kidneys, slice and remove any fat and skin. Drizzle with lemon juice or vinegar and leave to stand for half an hour.

After this time, place in a sieve or metal colander and scald by lowering into a pan with boiling water for half a minute. Remove and leave to dry.

Chop the onion, garlic and parsley and fry in hot oil. Scald and peel the tomato, chop and add to the onion when it begins to brown. Cook for 10 minutes. Season with salt and add the crushed pine kernels, the yolk of a hardboiled egg (mixed with a little water), and half a teaspoonful of paprika. Pour in a glass of white wine and leave to cook for 10 minutes before straining.

Season the kidneys with salt and sauté in a frying pan with hot oil for 8 minutes. Finally, add the kidneys to the sauce and heat, without bringing to the boil.

Serve hot, sprinkled with chopped parsley.

SAN JACOBO
HAM AND CHEESE FRITTERS

Ingredients

Makes 4 fritters:
- 8 small, thin beef fillets
- 4 slices cooked ham
- 4 slices cheese
- 4 asparagus
- 100 g (4 oz) mushrooms
- 1 clove garlic
- 1 small tin red bell peppers (*pimiento morrón*)
- 1 egg
- Breadcrumbs
- White wine
- Olive oil
- Salt

Preparation

Lightly salt the beef. Take a fillet and place a slice of ham on top, followed by a slice of cheese and an asparagus or two. Cover with another beef fillet.

Taking care to make sure the filling does not ooze out, dip both sides of the fritter in egg and coat in breadcrumbs.

Fry in hot oil until both sides are golden brown. Remove and place in an ovenproof dish.

Chop the garlic, clean and slice the mushrooms and dice the pepper. Strain the oil used for the fritters and use a little to fry the garlic. When it begins to brown, add the mushrooms and pepper. Add half a glass of wine, season with salt and simmer for 3 minutes.

Pour this mixture over the fritters and place in a preheated oven at a medium heat for 5 minutes.

Serve hot.

TERNERA ASADA
ROAST BEEF

Ingredients

- 1 kg (2 lb) rumpsteak
- 2 onions
- 4 cloves garlic
- White wine
- Olive oil
- Salt

Preparation

Crush two cloves of garlic in a mortar and use to rub over the beef. Leave to stand for half an hour, then season with salt.

In a cake tin, heat a generous amount of oil until it begins to smoke, and brown the meat evenly all over.

Roughly chop the onion, slice two cloves of garlic in half, and add to the meat. Fry for 4 minutes, then pour a glass of white wine over the beef. Cook on a low heat for an hour and a half. The meat is done when a larding needle can be pushed in easily.

Remove the meat and leave to cool. Strain the sauce through a colander.

The meat will keep for several days in the fridge. Serve in thin slices, either hot or cold. As a hot dish, add to the sauce and bring to the boil before serving, with red peppers and mashed potatoes on the side.

As a cold dish, serve the meat on its own with mayonnaise or a sauce of your choice.

TERNERA GOBERNADA
BEEF WITH PEAS

Ingredients

- 750 g (1½ lb) beef or veal
- 1 large onion
- 2 cloves garlic
- White wine
- Paprika
- Peas
- Red bell pepper (*pimiento morrón*)
- Brandy
- Olive oil
- Salt

Preparation

Cut the beef into fairly large pieces. Crush the garlic in a mortar and use to rub over the meat. Leave to stand for an hour.

Season with salt and brown in a casserole dish with hot oil. Remove the meat and use the oil to fry the onion (chopped) until it browns. Add the meat again, and a teaspoonful of paprika, half a glass of white wine and a squirt of brandy. Cook until the meat is tender and can be pierced easily with a larding needle.

Add peas. If they are fresh, they will need to be cooked for 20 minutes, though if they are tinned they can be added straight to the meat. Cook for a further 5 minutes.

Serve with the red peppers on the side.

TIRITAS DE TERNERA A LA MESONERA
BREADED BEEF STRIPS

Ingredients

- 3 beef or veal fillets
- 1 onion
- 2 cloves garlic
- Bay leaf
- Black pepper
- White wine
- 1 egg
- Breadcrumbs
- Meat stock
- Olive oil
- Salt

Preparation

Cut the fillets into strips 5 cm long and 1 cm ($1/2$ in) wide. Season the meat, dip in egg and coat in breadcrumbs.

Fry in hot oil until golden brown, then place in a casserole dish.

Strain the oil and use to sauté the chopped onion and garlic, together with a bay leaf. When the onion browns, add half a glass of wine and half a glass of stock, bring to the boil and pour over the meat. Cook for a further 5 minutes.

Serve with chips.

ALBÓNDIGAS DE BONITO
TUNA BALLS

Ingredients

- 1 kg (2 lb) bonito or tuna
- 150 g (5 oz) cured ham (jamón serrano)
- 1 tin red bell peppers (pimiento morrón)
- 2 cloves garlic
- 1 onion
- 1 egg
- 1 hardboiled egg
- Stale bread
- Flour
- White wine
- Olive oil
- Salt
- Parsley
- 1 tin pitted olives

Preparation

Remove the skin and any bones from the tuna. Chop finely, and season with salt, garlic and parsley, previously crushed in a mortar. Leave to marinade in a deep dish. Chop the ham, pepper, hardboiled egg and olives, and add to the fish. Soak the bread in milk, rinse and add to the mixture, together with a beaten egg. Knead with your hands to form a homogeneous mix. If it fails to bind, sprinkle with flour and knead again. Use your hands to form balls, and coat in flour.

Heat olive oil in a frying pan and fry the balls until golden brown.

Strain the oil used to fry the balls and heat in a casserole dish. Chop the onion and add to the pan. Crush a clove of garlic and a few sprigs of parsley in a mortar and pour in a glass of white wine. Pour into the casserole and add the fish balls. Cook on a low heat for 25 minutes before removing from the heat and straining the sauce through a sieve.

Can be served hot in their sauce, or cold with mayonnaise.

ALMEJAS A LA MARINERA
CLAMS WITH GARLIC

Ingredients

- 1 kg (2 lb) clams
- 1 large onion
- 4 cloves garlic
- White wine
- Breadcrumbs
- Parsley
- Chilli pepper
- Olive oil
- Salt

Preparation

Wash the clams several times by scrubbing them in cold water. Discard any dead clams (tap the open shells lightly; the dead clams will not close). Any clams that do not open once cooked should also be discarded.

Finely chop the onion and garlic and fry gently on a low heat in a casserole dish (earthenware if possible) with olive oil until the onion softens. Add a spoonful of fresh parsley crushed in a mortar, a tablespoonful of breadcrumbs, the chilli pepper and a glass and a half of white wine. Season with salt and boil for three minutes. Add the clams and cover the pan until the shells open.

Add water to the sauce if it is too thick, and breadcrumbs if it is too thin.

Serve piping hot in the same casserole dish.

ALMEJAS RELLENAS
STUFFED CLAMS

Ingredients

- 300 g (10 oz) clams
- 50 g (2 oz) cured ham (*jamón serrano*)
- Onion
- Parsley
- 1 egg yolk
- Flour
- Breadcrumbs
- Butter
- Olive oil

Preparation

Wash the clams several times by scrubbing with cold water and leaving them to soak to purge any sand. Remove any dead clams and any that do not close when tapped on the shell. Once cooked, discard any that do not open.

Cook the clams in a little water until the shells open. Strain the water and put to one side.

Finely chop half an onion and fry gently in oil (not too hot). Dice the ham, chop the parsley and clams, and add to the onion when it begins to brown. Stir in a teaspoonful of flour and slowly add the clam stock, stirring constantly. When the sauce has roughly the same consistency as a béchamel, add an egg yolk and stir well.

Fill one half of the clam shells with the mixture and sprinkle with breadcrumbs. Place in an ovenproof dish and grill to lightly toast the breadcrumbs.

Serve hot.

ANCHOAS RELLENAS
STUFFED ANCHOVIES

Ingredients

- 500 g (1 lb) fresh anchovies
- 1 onion
- 1 red pepper
- 1 green pepper
- Flour
- Egg
- Olive oil
- Salt

Preparation

Gut the anchovies by opening the fish and leaving it flat; now pull from the head down, removing the spine from the flesh. Wash the anchovies in cold water, dry well and season lightly.

Finely chop the onion and pepper and fry until soft.

Take an anchovy and cover it with the fried vegetables, placing a second anchovy on top, like a sandwich.

Roll the 'sandwich' in flour and dip in egg. Fry in very hot olive oil and place on kitchen paper to absorb any surplus oil.

Serve hot.

BACALAO AL AJO ARRIERO
COD WITH GARLIC

Ingredients

- 400 g (13 oz) salt cod
- 1 onion
- 3 cloves garlic
- Tomato sauce
- 1 sweet red pepper (*pimiento choricero*)
- Chilli pepper
- Olive oil
- Salt

Preparation

Leave the cod to soak in cold water for 36 to 48 hours, depending on its thickness, to remove the salt, changing the water several times. After this time, remove the skin and bones and chop the fish into small pieces.

In a saucepan with water, cook the skin and bones for 5 minutes to prepare a stock.

Chop the onion, slice the garlic and sauté gently in a frying pan. Soak the peppers in water, remove the flesh and add to the pan when the onion begins to brown, together with a touch of chilli and 6 tablespoonfuls of tomato sauce. When it begins to cook, add the cod, fry briefly and add a little stock. Cook on a low heat for 10 minutes.

Serve hot.

BACALAO ENCEBOLLADO
COD WITH ONIONS

Ingredients

- 250 g (8 oz) salt cod
- 1 green pepper
- 1 onion
- Chilli pepper (optional)
- Olive oil

Preparation

To desalt the cod, soak in various changes of water for 36-48 hours, depending on the thickness of the fish. Remove the skin and bones and cut into pieces.

Slice the onion into rings and the pepper in strips, and poach gently in oil. When they are done, add the cod and cook on a low heat for 10 minutes. Add a few rings of chilli pepper, to taste.

Serve the cod and vegetables on slices of bread.

BACALAO A LA VIZCAÍNA
BISCAY-STYLE COD

Ingredients

- 500 g (1 lb) salt cod
- 4 sweet red peppers (*pimiento choricero*)
- 1 hardboiled egg yolk
- 2 onions
- 1 slice fried bread
- 2 cloves garlic
- 6 almonds
- Olive oil

Preparation

Desalt the cod in various changes of cold water for 36-48 hours, depending on the thickness of the fish. Carefully remove the skin and bones, making sure the flesh remains intact. Cut into pieces, dry with a cloth and place in an earthenware casserole dish.

Place the peppers in hot water to soak.

Chop the onion, halve the garlic, and sauté gently until the onion is half cooked and half fried, without letting it brown. Remove the peppers from the water, scrape off the flesh and add to the onion.

In a mortar, crush the fried bread, egg yolk and almonds, and add a few drops of water. Add to the sauce and simmer for a couple more minutes. Strain through a colander if you prefer a thinner sauce.

Pour over the cod and cook on a low heat for 20 minutes.

Serve in the same earthenware dish.

BERBERECHOS CON VERDURAS
COCKLES WITH VEGETABLES

Ingredients

- 1 kg (2 lb) cockles
- 1 leek
- 1 carrot
- 1 onion
- 1 clove garlic
- 1 bay leaf
- White wine
- Olive oil
- Parsley
- Salt

Preparation

Wash the cockles in plenty of water by scrubbing one against another, discarding any that are dead (tap the open shells lightly; the dead cockles will not close). Any cockles that do not open once cooked should also be discarded.

Finely chop the onion, leek, carrot and garlic. In a casserole dish (earthenware if possible), fry the vegetables in olive oil until they brown, and add a bay leaf, a few sprigs of parsley crushed in a mortar and a glass and a half of white wine. Season with salt and boil for three minutes, then add the cockles and cover until the shells open.

Serve piping hot in the same casserole dish.

BOCADITOS DE LENGUADO
SOLE SNACKS

Ingredients

- 4 sole fillets (very thin)
- 2 slices cured ham
  (jamón serrano)
- 8 clams
- 8 prawns (gambas)
- Onion
- 1 clove garlic
- Parsley
- 1 egg
- Flour
- White wine
- Olive oil
- Salt

Preparation

Cut the sole and the ham into 4 x 6 cm (1¹/₂ x 2¹/₂ in) pieces.

On each piece of fish place a slice of ham, followed by a raw peeled prawn cut lengthways. Cover with another piece of fish, to form a mini sandwich.

Coat the fish snacks in flour and dip in egg, then fry in hot oil until brown on both sides. Remove from the pan and place in a casserole dish.

Finely chop half an onion and fry in the same oil. Crush garlic and parsley in a mortar, mix with half a glass of white wine and add to the pan when the onion is tender. Boil for a minute and pour over the fish. Wash the clams in water, add them to the casserole and cook for three minutes.

Serve hot.

BONITO ENCEBOLLADO
TUNA IN ONION

Ingredients

- 1 kg (2 lb) bonito or tuna
- 2 onions
- 3 cloves garlic
- Parsley
- Lemon
- 3 sweet red peppers (*pimiento choricero*)
- Stock
- Olive oil
- Salt
- Pepper

Preparation

Remove the skin and any bones from the tuna. Cut into even pieces and season with salt, pepper and a few drops of lemon juice. Leave to marinate.

Meanwhile, slice the onion into rings, chop the garlic, and fry in olive oil. Add a glass of stock, half a glass of water and chopped parsley, and reduce the sauce until it thickens.

Soak the peppers in hot water. Once tender, scrape off the flesh and add to the pan, stirring well for three minutes. Add the tuna pieces and leave to cook for a further five minutes.

Serve hot in the sauce, which can be strained through a sieve if so desired.

BOQUERONES EN VINAGRE
ANCHOVIES IN VINEGAR

Ingredients

- 300 g (10 oz) anchovies
- Wine vinegar
- Garlic
- Fresh parsley
- Salt
- Olive oil

Preparation

To clean the fish, run your index finger along the belly, completely opening the anchovy. Pull down gently from the head and separate the spine from the flesh. Wash the fish well in cold water and allow to dry. Divide each anchovy into two fillets.

Place the anchovies in a container and cover with vinegar. Leave to marinate for two to three hours until the flesh softens.

Meanwhile, finely chop the garlic and parsley, which should always be fresh. After the marinade time, rinse the anchovies well, removing all the liquid.

Place them on a platter, sprinkle with the garlic and parsley, and season with salt. Finally, drizzle with olive oil until they are covered.

BROCHETAS DE MARISCO
SEAFOOD BROCHETTES

Ingredients

- 6 mussels
- 6 *langostino* prawns
- 6 pieces white fish
- 6 mushrooms
- 1 green pepper
- 1 lemon
- 1 clove garlic
- Parsley
- Olive oil
- Salt

Preparation

Use a knife to scrape the mussel shells, rinse well in plenty of water, then steam the mussels in a pan until the shells open. Leave to cool and remove the mussels from their shells.

Peel the prawns and remove the heads. Cut the fish into cubes, removing any bones.

Chop the mushrooms and pepper into similar sized pieces.

Form the brochettes by inserting alternate ingredients onto skewers. Season and sprinkle with finely chopped garlic and parsley. Drizzle with the oil and lemon juice.

Grill until the fish and seafood are cooked.

BUÑUELOS DE BACALAO
COD PUFFS

Ingredients

- 250 g (8 oz) salt cod
- 200 g (7 oz) flour
- Beer
- Baking powder
- Olive oil
- Salt

Preparation

Desalt the cod by soaking it in several changes of water for 36-48 hours, depending on the thickness. Remove the skin and bones and cut into pieces.

Prepare the batter by mixing the flour, baking powder and salt in a bowl. Add beer and mix to form a thick cream.

Sauté the fish in a frying pan with a little olive oil. Add the cod to the bowl and mix well.

Use a spoon to pick out the fish pieces and fry in hot oil until golden brown.

Serve straight away.

CALAMARES ENCEBOLLADOS

SQUID IN ONION

Ingredients

- 4 medium squid
- 2 onions
- 1 green pepper
- Parsley
- 1 lemon
- Olive oil
- Salt

Preparation

This recipe only requires the sac or body of the squid.

To clean the squid, pull the head to remove it from the body. Remove the innards and the quill from inside, and the dark skin covering the squid. Open the squid lengthways with scissors to produce a kind of fillet. Wash in cold water and dry.

Chop the onion into slices and the pepper into strips. Fry in hot olive oil until cooked through.

Meanwhile, spread the squid with olive oil and lemon juice and griddle in a separate frying pan until golden brown on both sides. Cut into pieces and sprinkle with salt and chopped parsley, and cover with the vegetables.

Serve hot.

CALAMARES FRITOS
FRIED SQUID RINGS

Ingredients

- 1 kg (2 lb) squid
- 3 cloves garlic
- Flour
- Olive oil
- Salt

Preparation

Clean the squid by pulling the head to separate it from the body. Use a knife to cut the tentacles above the eyes. Make sure you have removed the tooth found inside the head. Remove the innards and quill, together with the skin covering the body. Wash the tentacles and body in cold water and dry.

Chop the squid into rings and leave to marinate for an hour in olive oil and chopped garlic. After this time remove the garlic and season the squid with a pinch of salt (though squid needs very little if any seasoning).

Coat each ring or strip in flour and fry in hot olive oil until golden brown.

Serve hot with chunks of lemon.

CÓCTEL DE GAMBAS
PRAWN COCKTAIL

Ingredients

- 500 g (1 lb) prawns
- Lettuce
- 2 eggs
- Olive oil
- Lemon
- Ketchup
- Brandy
- White pepper
- Salt

Preparation

Cook the prawns for a minute or two in salted boiling water. Remove from the water and place in cold water before peeling and removing the heads.

Wash and finely chop the lettuce heart.

Prepare a mayonnaise with the eggs, olive oil, the juice of half a lemon and salt.

In a bowl, mix the mayonnaise with two or three tablespoonfuls of ketchup, a dash of brandy and pepper.

Place the lettuce and prawns in champagne or cocktail glasses and cover with the sauce. Decorate with two or three prawns.

Place in the fridge and serve chilled.

CREPES DE MARISCO
SEAFOOD CRÊPES

Ingredients

- Milk
- Baking powder
- 5 eggs
- Flour
- 250 g (8 oz) *langostino* prawns
- 1 hardboiled egg
- 10 crab sticks
- Onion
- 1 lettuce heart
- 1 lemon
- Brandy
- Ketchup
- Olive oil
- Salt

Preparation

In a pan with half a litre of warm milk, a pinch of salt and half a teaspoonful of baking powder, dilute the flour to form a batter that should be light and creamy, but still with a certain consistency and lump-free. Beat four eggs and add to the batter. Leave to stand for at least half an hour.

Heat a few drops of oil in a small frying pan, and when it is hot pour in a small amount of the batter to cover the base of the pan and form very thin pancakes. Brown them on both sides, remove and put to one side.

Cook the prawns in salted boiling water for two or three minutes. Remove from the pan and place in cold water before peeling and removing the heads.

Prepare the following mayonnaise: place an egg, salt and the juice of the lemon in the jug of a hand blender. Use the blender to mix the ingredients, slowly adding the oil to form the mayonnaise. Finally blend in a little ketchup and a squirt of brandy.

Finely chop the prawns, crab sticks, boiled egg, half an onion and lettuce and place in a bowl. Mix with the mayonnaise, spread over the crêpes and roll them up.

Arrange on a platter and serve cold.

CROISSANTS RELLENOS DE MARISCO
SEAFOOD-FILLED CROISSANTS

Ingredients

- 6 croissants
- 150 g (5 oz) prawns
- 10 crab sticks
- 1 hardboiled egg
- 1 lettuce heart
- 1 egg
- 1 lemon
- Olive oil
- Salt

Preparation

Cook the prawns in salted boiling water for a minute or two. Remove from the pan and place in cold water before peeling and removing the heads. Put 6 peeled prawns to one side.

Prepare a mayonnaise: place an egg, the juice of a lemon and salt in a bowl. Mix with the blender, slowly adding olive oil to form the mayonnaise.

Finely chop the lettuce, cooked prawns, crab sticks and hardboiled egg and place in a bowl. Mix with the mayonnaise.

Slice open the croissants and fill with the mixture.

Place a whole prawn inside each croissant so that it is visible.

CROQUETAS DE PESCADO
FISH CROQUETTES

Ingredients

- 200 g (7 oz) hake
  (or any other white fish)
- 200 g (7 oz) prawns
- 1 onion
- Parsley
- Butter
- Flour
- Olive oil
- Breadcrumbs
- 1 egg
- Milk
- Salt

Preparation

Cook the prawns in salted water for a minute or two. Strain and put the water to one side. Cook the fish in water with salt, the peel of an onion and a few sprigs of parsley for 15 minutes. Once cooked, strain the water, add part of this stock to the prawn water and put to one side.

Peel and chop the prawns. Flake the fish, discarding the skin and bones.

Chop the onion and fry in a little oil until brown, add the fish and prawns and sauté for a minute or so.

In a casserole dish, melt two tablespoonfuls of butter and add four or five of flour. Add the milk and part of the cooking water, bit by bit, stirring well with a wooden spoon to prevent any lumps from forming. Leave to cook until the béchamel thickens. Season with salt and add the prawns and fish, mixing well.

Spread over a platter and leave to cool.

Once it is cold, mould the paste with your hands to form the croquettes. Coat each one in breadcrumbs, dip in egg and roll in breadcrumbs. Fry in plenty of hot oil until golden brown.

CHIPIRONES EN SU TINTA
CUTTLEFISH IN THEIR INK

Ingredients

- 1 kg (2 lb) cuttlefish
- 1 onion
- 2 tomatoes
- Parsley
- 2 cloves garlic
- Olive oil
- White wine
- 2 sacs squid ink
- Salt

Preparation

Remove the heads from the cuttlefish and use a knife to cut the tentacles above the eyes. Remove the innards and quill from the body. Wash in cold water and rinse. Chop the tentacles and the body into pieces (not too small, as they shrink considerably when cooked).

Finely chop the onion and garlic and fry in olive oil. Meanwhile, scald the tomatoes in boiling water for two minutes to make them easier to peel. Dice the tomatoes and add to the onion when it begins to brown, together with the chopped parsley. Stir for a moment and add the cuttlefish. Fry for two minutes and add half a glass of white wine. Cover and simmer on a medium heat for thirty minutes, then add the ink mixed with a little water. Add salt if necessary, though the ink generally contains sufficient, and in any case cuttlefish need very little salt. Leave to cook for a further five minutes.

Serve hot with chips or boiled rice.

CHIPIRONES RELLENOS
STUFFED CUTTLEFISH

Ingredients

- 1 kg (2 lb) cuttlefish
- 100 g (4 oz) cured ham (jamón serrano)
- 2 tomatoes
- 1 onion
- 3 cloves garlic
- Parsley
- White wine
- 2 hardboiled eggs
- 2 sacs squid ink
- Olive oil
- Salt

Preparation

Clean the cuttlefish by removing the head from the body, cut off and chop the tentacles. Chop the ham into small pieces.

Chop half an onion and fry in hot olive oil. When it begins to brown, add the ham and the chopped hardboiled eggs. Crush two cloves of garlic and the parsley in a mortar, together with a dash of white wine, and add to the pan. Stir until it begins to boil, and add the tentacles. Check for salt and leave to cook for two or three minutes. Allow to cool.

Use this mixture to stuff the cuttlefish, and close them with a toothpick to prevent the stuffing from oozing out.

Chop the other onion half, a few sprigs of parsley and a clove of garlic, and fry in a casserole dish with olive oil. Peel and chop the tomatoes and add to the onion. Cook briefly, then add the cuttlefish and stir. Add half a glass of white wine, cover and simmer for 20 minutes. Add the ink and cook for a further 20 minutes. Finally, strain the sauce and pour over the cuttlefish.

Serve hot.

GAMBAS AL AJILLO
PRAWNS IN GARLIC

Ingredients

- 500 g (1 lb) fresh prawns
- 2 chilli peppers
- 6 cloves garlic
- Olive oil
- Salt

Preparation

Remove the heads and skin of the prawns, as well as the intestine or black string that runs along the belly. Wash the prawns in cold water and dry well.

Cut the chilli pepper into rings and remove the seeds. Chop the garlic.

Heat olive oil in a frying pan (an earthenware casserole is even better), fry the garlic, and when it begins to brown, add the chilli and the prawns. Season lightly and fry for a couple of minutes, stirring well until the prawns are cooked.

Serve while it is still sizzling hot.

GAMBAS CON BECHAMEL
PRAWNS IN BÉCHAMEL

Ingredients

- Prawns
- Flour
- Milk
- Butter
- Salt
- Egg
- Breadcrumbs
- Olive oil

Preparation

Rinse the raw prawns, peel and remove the heads, and salt lightly.

Skewer the prawns two by two on toothpicks and put to one side.

Prepare the béchamel: melt a tablespoonful of butter in a bowl and add two tablespoonfuls of flour, stirring with a wooden spoon. Add the milk slowly, stirring continuously to prevent lumps from forming. Season with salt.

When the sauce is cooked, coat the prawns and leave to cool.

Use your hands to form round balls with each skewer. Dip in egg and coat in breadcrumbs. Fry in plenty of hot oil until golden brown.

Serve hot.

GAMBAS REBOZADAS (Gambas con gabardina)
PRAWNS IN BATTER (Prawns in overcoats)

Ingredients

- 250 g (8 oz) prawns
- 150 g (5 oz) flour
- Beer
- Saffron
- Baking powder
- Olive oil
- Salt

Preparation

Rinse the uncooked prawns, peel and remove the head, but leave the tail. Season lightly with salt.

In a bowl mix the flour, a tablespoonful of yeast, salt and a pinch of ground saffron. Stir in beer to obtain a thick cream.

Heat plenty of olive oil in a frying pan. Pick up each prawn by the tail and dip into the batter until evenly coated. With the prawn still in your hands, and with the help of a spoon, fry in the hot oil, making sure that the prawns do not stick together.

Serve freshly fried.

MEJILLONES A LA MARINERA
MUSSELS À LA MARINIÈRE

Ingredients

- 1.5 kg (3 lb) mussels
- 1 onion
- 2 cloves garlic
- Parsley
- Breadcrumbs
- 1 chilli pepper
- White wine
- Olive oil
- Salt

Preparation

Scrape the mussel shells with a knife, and remove the beards. Discard any mussels with broken shells and any which, when open, do not close when tapped. Rinse in plenty of cold water.

Chop the onion and sauté in a casserole with hot olive oil. When it begins to brown, add a tablespoonful of breadcrumbs and a chilli pepper. Crush two cloves of garlic and a few sprigs of parsley in a mortar, together with a glass of white wine, and add to the onion. Season with a pinch of salt, bring to the boil and add the mussels. Cover and cook for ten minutes.

Serve hot.

MEJILLONES A LA VINAGRETA
MUSSELS IN VINAIGRETTE

Ingredients

- 1.5 kg (3 lb) mussels
- 1 onion
- 1 tin red bell peppers (*pimiento morrón*)
- Parsley
- 1 hardboiled egg
- Vinegar
- Olive oil
- Salt

Preparation

Scrape the mussel shells with a knife, and remove the beards. Rinse well in cold water, discarding any mussels with broken shells or which, when open, do not close when tapped.

Bring a glass of unsalted water to a lively boil, add the mussels and cover the pan. Remove from the heat once all the shells have opened. Remove from the water and leave to cool.

Remove and discard the empty shell from each mussel, leaving the other half with the mussel inside. Arrange on a platter.

Prepare the vinaigrette: place a glass of olive oil, vinegar and a little salt in a deep bowl and whisk until creamy. Finely chop the onion, pepper, parsley and hardboiled egg, and add to the dressing, stirring well. Add more salt and vinegar if necessary.

Pour a spoonful of the dressing over each mussel, and serve cold.

MEJILLONES RELLENOS
STUFFED MUSSELS

Ingredients

- 1.5 kg (3 lb) mussels
- 150 g (5 oz) cured ham (jamón serrano)
- Onion
- Butter
- Flour
- Milk
- 1 egg
- Breadcrumbs
- Olive oil
- Salt

Preparation

Clean the mussels by scraping their shells with a knife and removing the beards. Wash well in cold water, discarding any mussels with broken shells and those which, when open, do not close when tapped.

Bring a glass of unsalted water to a lively boil, add the mussels and cover the pan. Cook until all the mussels open, remove from the pan and leave to cool.

Remove all the shells, putting aside half a shell for each mussel. Chop the mussels into three or four pieces.

Chop half an onion and sauté with a little olive oil. When it begins to brown, add the chopped ham and the mussel pieces, and put to one side.

In a saucepan, melt the butter and add the flour, stirring with a wooden spoon, and then slowly add the milk. Season with salt and cook for ten minutes, stirring continuously. Add the mussels, stir well and use this mixture to fill the mussel shells. Allow to cool. Dip the shells in egg and then in breadcrumbs before frying in plenty of hot oil.

Serve piping hot.

PASTEL DE MEJILLONES
MUSSEL PIE

Ingredients

- 2 kg (4 lb) mussels
- 1/2 green pepper
- 1/2 red pepper
- 1 onion
- 4 eggs
- Single cream
- Butter
- Olive oil
- Salt

Preparation

Scrape the mussels with a knife and rinse in cold water. Cook in a little water until they open. Remove from the shells and put to one side.

Finely chop the onion and peppers and sauté gently in oil until browned. Chop the mussels, add to the pan and cook for a minute or so. Spoon into a large bowl and add the eggs, a cup of cream and a pinch of salt. Blend the mixture and pour into a mould greased with butter.

Place in the oven in a bain marie at a medium heat for around 40 minutes, until it sets.

Allow to cool before removing from the mould.

PASTEL DE PESCADO
FISH LOAF

Ingredients

- 1 kg (2 lb) white fish
- 200 g (7 oz) prawns (*gambas* or *langostinos*)
- 1 leek
- 1 carrot
- Onion
- Parsley
- Single cream
- 150 g (5 oz) tomato sauce
- 5 eggs
- Butter
- Pepper
- Salt

Preparation

Cook the fish with the leek, carrot, a piece of onion, parsley and salt for 15 minutes.

Cook the prawns for a minute or two in boiling water with salt. Remove from the pan, place in a bowl to cool, then peel and remove the heads.

Flake the fish into small pieces, taking care to remove the skin and bones. Discard the vegetables.

In a bowl, mix a glass of cream with the tomato sauce, the eggs and prawns. Season with salt and pepper and blend. Add the fish, mix well and turn out into a mould greased with butter. Cover with tinfoil and place in the oven in a bain marie on a medium heat for 45 minutes.

Leave to cool before removing from the mould.

Serve cold with toast and mayonnaise.

PATÉ DE SALMÓN
SALMON PÂTÉ

Ingredients

- 4 slices salmon
- 200 g (7 oz) prawns
- 8 mussels
- Single cream
- 150 g (5 oz) tomato sauce
- 5 eggs
- Butter
- Pepper
- Salt

Preparation

Sprinkle the salmon with salt and grill, removing before it cooks completely. Remove the skin and bones. Grill the prawns and then remove the heads and shells.

Steam the mussels until they open.

Mix together the eggs, a glass of cream, the tomato sauce, mussels and prawns. Season with salt and pepper and mix with the blender. Flake the salmon in small pieces and add to the mix, stirring well.

Grease a mould with butter and pour in the mixture. Cover with tinfoil and place in the oven in a bain marie on a medium heat for 45 minutes. Use a larding needle to check the pâté has set.

Leave to cool before removing from the mould.

Serve cold with mayonnaise, chopped lettuce and toast.

PINCHOS DE MAR REBOZADOS
SEAFOOD SKEWERS IN BATTER

Ingredients

- 15 medium prawns
- 15 mussels
- 1 egg
- Flour
- Breadcrumbs
- Olive oil
- Black pepper
- Salt

Preparation

Wash the mussels in plenty of water, scraping the shells to remove any barnacles.

Cook the mussels in a casserole dish with a glass of water (do not add salt) until the shells open. Remove and discard the shells once cold, and put to one side.

Rinse the raw prawns, peel and remove the heads, and salt lightly.

Use toothpicks to make the skewers, alternating prawns and mussels. Add the tiniest pinch of salt and ground pepper, then coat in flour, dip in egg, and finally roll in breadcrumbs.

Fry the skewers in plenty of hot oil until golden brown all over. Remove and place on kitchen roll to absorb the oil.

Serve hot.

Ideal accompanied with a tartar sauce.

PULPO A FEIRA
GALICIA-STYLE OCTOPUS

Ingredients

- 1 octopus
- 1 bay leaf
- Paprika/cayenne pepper
- Olive oil
- Salt

Preparation

Scrub the octopus well in cold water to clean it. Using a pestle, beat the suckers to free any sand. Scrub again until completely clean.

Once dried, the octopus should be placed in the freezer for two to three days to tenderise the meat. After this time, remove from the freezer and defrost.

Cook the octopus in boiling water with a bay leaf until tender (check with a fork). The cooking time will depend on the size of the octopus. Once tender, remove from the pan and leave to cool.

Chop the octopus into slices with scissors and season with salt and paprika or cayenne pepper (to taste), and drizzle with olive oil.

Boiled potatoes make an ideal accompaniment.

Serve on a wooden board, if possible.

PULPO A LA CAZUELA
OCTOPUS CASSEROLE

Ingredients

- 1 large octopus
- 1 pepper
- 2 tomatoes
- 1 onion
- 3 cloves garlic
- 400 g (13 oz) potatoes
- Parsley
- Bay leaf
- Olive oil
- Salt
- Pepper

Preparation

Wash the octopus well by scrubbing it in cold water, making sure there is no sand (particularly in the suckers). Place in the freezer for two or three days to tenderise the meat.

Defrost the octopus and cook in boiling water with a bay leaf until tender (a fork should pierce the flesh easily).

Remove from the pan and put to one side to cool.

Finely chop the onion and pepper and fry in an earthenware casserole with hot olive oil until tender. Chop the tomatoes and crush the garlic in a mortar with a few sprigs of parsley, and add to the casserole. Season with salt and pepper. Chop the octopus, add to the mixture and leave to cook for ten minutes, stirring occasionally.

Meanwhile, peel and wash the potatoes, dice and fry in hot olive oil. Add to the octopus at the last moment, as otherwise they could thicken the sauce.

Serve in the same earthenware dish.

PULPO A LA VINAGRETA
OCTOPUS IN VINAIGRETTE DRESSING

Ingredients

- 1 octopus
- 1 bay leaf
- 1 onion
- Parsley
- 2 hardboiled eggs
- 1 tin red bell peppers
  (pimiento morrón)
- Vinegar
- Olive oil
- Salt

Preparation

Wash the octopus carefully by scrubbing it in plenty of cold water, making sure that the suckers are free of sand. Place the octopus in the freezer for two or three days to tenderise the meat.

Defrost the octopus and place in a pan with boiling water and a bay leaf. Cook until tender (check by pricking with a fork). Cooking time will depend on the size of the octopus. Remove from the water and leave to cool.

Prepare the dressing as follows: in a bowl mix twelve tablespoonfuls of olive oil, four of vinegar and a pinch of salt. Beat well to produce a creamy mixture. Finely chop a small onion, a few sprigs of parsley, the pepper and the hardboiled eggs, and mix in to the dressing. Check for salt and vinegar to taste.

Serve the octopus in slices, with the dressing poured over the top.

REVUELTO DE ORICIOS (Erizos de Mar)
SCRAMBLED EGGS WITH SEA URCHINS

Ingredients

- 2 dozen sea urchins
- 6 eggs
- Single cream
- Olive oil
- Salt

Preparation

Place the urchins in boiling water for half an hour, then remove and allow to cool. Use a spoon to open, from the middle out. Extract the orange-coloured eggs and discard the rest.

Lightly beat the eggs, together with salt and half a cup of cream. Add the urchin eggs, taking care not to break them, and mix well.

Gently heat oil in a frying pan and pour in the mixture, stirring until the egg has almost set.

Serve sprinkled with chopped parsley.

ROLLITOS DE SALMÓN
SALMON ROLLS

Ingredients

- 100 g (4 oz) smoked salmon
- 8 crab sticks
- 15 prawns
- Onion
- 1 hardboiled egg
- 1 egg
- Lemon
- Sliced bread
- Olive oil
- Salt

Preparation

Cook the prawns in salted boiling water for a minute or two. Remove and place in cold water before peeling and removing the heads.

Prepare a mayonnaise by placing an egg, the juice of a lemon and salt in the jug of a hand blender. Begin to blend, slowly adding oil until the mayonnaise is thick enough.

Chop the prawns, crab sticks, hardboiled egg and half an onion, and place in a bowl. Mix the ingredients with plenty of mayonnaise.

Spread the slices of salmon out and place two or three teaspoonfuls of the mixture on each one. Wrap them up in the shape of rolls and place on pieces of lightly toasted bread.

SALPICÓN DE MARISCO
SEAFOOD SALAD

Ingredients

- 500 g (1 lb) hake
- 500 g (1 lb) monkfish
- 500 g (1 lb) Norway lobster (cigala)
- 500 g (1 lb) prawns (gambas)
- 200 g (7 oz) large prawns (langostinos)
- Onion
- Parsley
- Vinegar
- Red bell pepper (pimiento morrón)
- 2 hardboiled eggs
- Olive oil
- Salt

Preparation

Place the fish, together with a piece of onion and a sprig of parsley, in a pan with salted cold water and cook for 10 to 15 minutes, then drain and leave to cool.

Cook the seafood in salted boiling water (one or two minutes for the gambas, and two to three minutes for the cigalas and langostinos). Cool with cold water and peel.

Chop the gambas and cigalas into small pieces. Put the langostinos to one side. Flake the fish, removing the bones and skin.

Mix the fish and seafood and cover with the vinaigrette dressing.

To prepare the dressing: place a glass of olive oil, vinegar and a pinch of salt in a deep bowl. Whisk until creamy. Finely chop the onion, pepper and hardboiled eggs and add to the bowl. Add more salt and vinegar if necessary.

Serve in a large platter or in individual dishes and adorn with the langostinos.

SARDINAS AL HORNO
ROAST SARDINES

Ingredients

- 2 dozen medium sardines
- 1 green pepper
- 1 onion
- 2 cloves garlic
- Parsley
- Breadcrumbs
- Olive oil
- Vinegar
- Salt

Preparation

First clean the sardines by inserting your finger in the belly and removing the innards. Open the sardine, and remove the head by separating the central spine from the flesh. The fish should remain completely open like a fillet. Wash in cold water and dry with a cloth. Season with salt.

Chop the onion and pepper into strips, slice the garlic and fry with a little olive oil. Once cooked, use the vegetables to line the bottom of an ovenproof dish and place the fillets on top, with the skin face up. Sprinkle with chopped parsley and breadcrumbs, and drizzle with a little olive oil and vinegar.

Place in the oven at a high heat for five minutes until cooked.

Serve hot.

SARDINAS EN ESCABECHE
PICKLED SARDINES

Ingredients

- 500 g (1 lb) medium sardines
- 2 cloves garlic
- Vinegar
- Flour
- Parsley
- Bay leaf
- Paprika
- Pepper
- Olive oil
- Salt

Preparation

Clean the sardines by removing the head and extracting the innards. Season lightly and coat in flour. Fry in hot oil until they brown, remove and place on a platter.

With the same oil used to fry the sardines, sauté the garlic, parsley and bay leaf. When the onion begins to brown, remove the pan from the heat and add the ground pepper, a teaspoonful of paprika and a small glass of vinegar. Cook for three minutes and cover the sardines with the sauce.

Leave to stand and serve cool.

The sardines will keep for several days in the fridge.

VIEIRAS GRATINADAS
SCALLOPS AU GRATIN

Ingredients

- 10 scallops
- Milk
- Butter
- Flour
- Breadcrumbs
- Parsley
- Salt

Preparation

Wash the scallops and leave them for a few hours in salted water to purge of any sand.

Place in a pan with a little boiling water until they open.

Remove the molluscs from the shells and put to one side, first removing the black edge around the flesh and eggs. Keep the deeper of the two shells, as well as the water used to open them.

Meanwhile, prepare the following béchamel sauce: in a saucepan, melt a tablespoonful of butter and add three tablespoonfuls of flour, stirring with a wooden spoon. Pour in half a glass of the cooking water, stirring constantly, and then slowly add the milk until the sauce thickens. Check for salt, add the scallops and cook for two to three minutes.

Grease the shells with butter and fill with the scallops and the sauce. Sprinkle with breadcrumbs and chopped parsley, and place under the grill to brown.

Serve straight away.

BARQUITO DE BERENJENAS CON CARNE
AUBERGINE AND MINCE BOATS

Ingredients

- 2 medium aubergines
- 200 g (7 oz) minced beef
- 1 red pepper
- 1 onion
- 3 cloves garlic
- 3 tomatoes
- 100 g (4 oz) mushrooms
- Grated cheese
- Thyme
- Olive oil
- Salt

Preparation

Wash the aubergines and slice in half lengthways. Scoop out the flesh with a knife, taking care not to break the skin but leaving the walls as thin as possible.

Chop the red pepper, onion and garlic and sauté in hot oil. Chop the aubergine flesh, peel and chop the tomatoes, slice the mushrooms and add to the pan. Season with salt and cook for 10 minutes, stirring occasionally.

Season the mince with salt and thyme and sauté in a second frying pan with a little oil. Add to the vegetables once browned. Use this mixture to stuff the aubergines, and cover with grated cheese.

Place the aubergine boats in a fish pan and grill for 5 minutes until golden brown.

Serve hot.

CARACOLES EN SALSA DE ALMENDRAS
SNAILS IN ALMOND SAUCE

Ingredients

- 600 g (1¼ lb) snails
- 100 g (4 oz) cured ham (*jamón serrano*)
- 250 g (8 oz) pork belly fat (*tocino*)
- 100 g (4 oz) ground almonds
- 1 sweet red pepper (*pimiento choricero*)
- 2 tomatoes
- 1 onion
- 1 clove garlic
- Parsley, Bay leaf
- Chilli
- Olive oil
- Salt

Preparation

Clean the snails well in plenty of cold water. Leave them to soak for two hours in water, salt and vinegar, rinsing several times, before cooking for 10 minutes. Rinse again several times until the smell of vinegar disappears.

Boil for 10 minutes in water, then rinse again with cold water.

Bring a pan of salted water to the boil and add the snails, together with a few pieces of onion, a clove of garlic, parsley and a bay leaf. Cook for an hour and a half. Drain well and place in an earthenware casserole dish.

Meanwhile, chop the onion and poach in oil. Peel and chop the tomatoes, and soak the pepper to remove the flesh, and add both to the onion when it begins to brown.

Dice the ham and pork fat and sauté in a second frying pan, then add to the tomato sauce. Stir in the almonds, half a glass of wine and a chilli pepper, bring to the boil and pour over the snails.

Cook for half an hour, adding water if necessary.

Serve hot, together with the sauce, in the same dish.

CREPES DE JAMÓN Y QUESO
HAM AND CHEESE CRÊPES

Ingredients

- Milk
- Baking powder
- 4 eggs
- Flour
- Onion
- 150 g (5 oz) wild mushrooms
- 200 g (7 oz) cooked ham
- 200 g (7 oz) creamy cheese
- Grated cheese
- Pepper
- Olive oil
- Salt

Preparation

In a pan with half a litre of warm milk, a pinch of salt and half a teaspoonful of baking powder, dilute the flour to form a batter, which should be light and creamy, but still with a certain consistency and lump-free. Leave to stand for at least half an hour.

Heat a few drops of oil in a small frying pan, and when it is hot pour in a small amount of the batter to cover the base of the pan, forming very thin pancakes. Brown them on both sides, remove and put to one side.

Finely chop half an onion and sauté in a frying pan. Clean and chop the mushrooms and add to the pan when the onion becomes transparent. Season with salt and pepper and cook until the juice evaporates.

Dice the ham and sauté in a second frying pan before adding to the mushrooms. Remove from the heat and grate the creamy cheese over the top, which should melt into a cream.

Spread a little filling over each crêpe, roll up and place in an ovenproof dish. Sprinkle with grated cheese and place in a warm oven until the cheese melts.

Serve straight away.

CROQUETAS DE JAMÓN
HAM CROQUETTES

Ingredients

- Flour
- Milk
- Nutmeg
- Butter
- 100 g (4 oz) cured ham
  (jamón serrano)
- Breadcrumbs
- 1 egg
- Olive oil
- Salt

Preparation

In a saucepan, melt two tablespoonfuls of butter and add five more of flour. When the roux begins to brown, slowly add the milk, stirring constantly with a wooden spoon to prevent lumps from forming. Leave to cook slowly, adding milk from time to time. Add salt and a pinch of nutmeg. Dice the ham, sauté in a little olive oil, and add to the pan. Continue stirring until the sauce is cooked.

Pour into a bowl and leave to cool for a few hours. Once cold, take a lump of the mixture and use your hands to make round or oval shapes. Coat in breadcrumbs, dip in egg and roll again in breadcrumbs.

Fry in plenty of hot oil.

Best served hot.

EMPANADILLAS ASTURIANAS
ASTURIAS-STYLE PASTIES

Ingredients

- 100 g (4 oz) cured ham (*jamón serrano*)
- 100 g (4 oz) chorizo
- 1 hardboiled egg
- Onion
- Tomato sauce
- White wine
- Olive oil
- Flour
- Salt

Preparation

Fry a few strips of lemon rind in half a glass of oil. Leave to cool before mixing with half a glass of white wine, add salt and whisk until milky. Add the flour gradually, stirring with a wooden spoon at first and then kneading until the dough does not stick to your hands. Leave to stand in a cool place for two hours.

Meanwhile prepare the filling: chop half an onion and fry in very little oil. When the onion begins to brown, add two or three tablespoonfuls of tomato sauce. Dice the ham and add to the pan, stir briefly and remove from the heat.

Before making the pasties, chop the chorizo and hardboiled egg and add to the filling.

Once the dough has stood for two hours, use a rolling pin on a floured surface to produce a fairly thin dough. Use a glass to cut circles into the dough. Place a little filling in each circle, and fold in half to form half-moons. Join the edges together by pressing down on them with a fork, so that the filling does not ooze out. Fry the pasties in hot oil until golden brown.

ENSALADILLA DE AGUACATE
AVOCADO SALAD

Ingredients

- 3 potatoes
- 4 eggs
- 1 avocado
- 1 apple
- 1 kiwi
- 100 g (4 oz) cooked ham
- 100 g (4 oz) creamy cheese
- Mayonnaise
- Salt

Preparation

Wash the potatoes and boil in plenty of salted water until they can be pierced easily with a larding needle. Boil three eggs for 12 minutes.

Remove the potatoes and eggs and allow to cool before peeling and shelling.

Meanwhile, prepare a mayonnaise by placing an egg, the juice of a lemon and a little water in the jug of a hand blender. Slowly add oil as you blend, until the sauce reaches the required thickness. Season with salt.

Dice the potatoes, two eggs, the fruit, ham and cheese. Mix all the ingredients together with the mayonnaise and arrange on a platter.

Serve sprinkled with grated hardboiled egg.

HOJALDRES DE CIRUELAS Y BACON
PRUNE AND BACON ROLLS

Ingredients

- 200 g (7 oz) fresh or frozen puff pastry
- 12 prunes, pitted
- 6 rashers bacon
- 1 egg

Preparation

Roll out the pastry and divide into rectangles approximately 8 by 4 cm (3 in x 1½ in). Cut the bacon into similar, slightly smaller shapes.

Wrap each prune in a piece of bacon, then wrap this in a piece of pastry. Roll the pastry up into a cylinder, wetting the edge with a little water and pressing down with your finger to close the roll.

Place the rolls on a baking tray, coat them with egg and place in a pre-heated oven on a medium heat until the pastry is cooked.

PINCHOS DE ANCHOAS
ANCHOVY TOASTS

Ingredients

- 2 tins anchovies in oil
- 10 prawns
- 1 green pepper
- 1 red pepper
- 1 onion
- Olive oil
- Salt

Preparation

Cut the peppers into quarters and fry in oil on a low heat. Slice the onion into half rings and poach.

Cook the prawns in salted boiling water for a minute or two. Remove from the water and place in cold water to cool, remove the head and peel.

On a piece of toast, first place a piece of green pepper (remove the skin), then two anchovies, leaving a space between them for the onion. Slice the red pepper into thin strips and place across the anchovies. Top with a prawn or two and serve.

PUDIN DE BONITO
TUNA PUDDING

Preparation

Wash the potatoes, without peeling, and boil in plenty of salted water.

Meanwhile, chop an onion and fry in hot olive oil. When it is brown, add four tablespoonfuls of tomato sauce and reduce until the sauce thickens.

Peel the potatoes and blend together with the tuna (drain off the oil), onion and tomato, and mix well.

Turn into a mould, previously greased with butter, and place in the fridge for six hours.

Serve cold with mayonnaise.

Ingredients

- 500 g (1 lb) potatoes
- 2 tins bonito or tuna in oil
- Tomato sauce
- 1 medium onion
- Olive oil
- Salt

QUICHE DE JAMÓN Y QUESO
CHEESE AND HAM QUICHE

Ingredients

- Fresh or frozen
  puff pastry
- 150 (5 oz) cooked ham
- 100 g (4 oz) creamy
  cheese
- 4 eggs
- Single cream
- Grated cheese
- Butter
- Salt

Preparation

Grease an oven mould with butter and line with the pastry.

On top of the pastry base place a layer of ham slices, a layer of sliced cheese, and a second layer of ham. Cover with grated cheese.

Beat two whole eggs and two egg yolks in a bowl, together with half a glass of cream and a pinch of salt. Pour this mixture over the quiche and place in a medium-hot oven for 30 minutes until the egg sets.

Remove from the oven, turn out the quiche and serve warm.

REVUELTO DE AJETES CON GAMBAS
SCRAMBLED EGGS WITH SPRING GARLIC AND PRAWNS

Ingredients

- 300 g (10 oz) prawns
- 300 g (10 oz) spring garlic (*ajetes*)
- 5 eggs
- Parsley
- Pepper
- Single cream
- Olive oil
- Salt

Preparation

Rinse and peel the raw prawns, discarding the heads. Sprinkle with salt.

Clean and chop the garlic and fry in a little oil. When they are almost cooked, add the prawns and sauté for two minutes. Season with salt, pepper and chopped parsley.

Beat the eggs and mix with two tablespoonfuls of cream. Season with salt and pour over the prawns and garlic. Stir until the eggs begin to set.

Serve hot with toast.

ROLLITOS DE REPOLLO
CABBAGE ROLLS

Ingredients

- 10 cabbage leaves
- 500 g (1 lb) minced beef
- 1 onion
- 2 carrots
- 1 pepper
- 3 cloves garlic
- Parsley
- White wine
- Meat stock
- Tomato sauce
- 2 eggs
- Flour
- Olive oil
- Salt

Preparation

Select the whitest cabbage leaves and place in boiling water for a minute. Drain and leave to cool.

Finely chop half an onion, together with the carrot, pepper and garlic, and sauté in a frying pan. Add the meat and stir until completely cooked. Add a dash of white wine and two tablespoonfuls of tomato sauce, and leave to cook for three minutes. Season with salt and remove from the heat. Beat an egg and stir in, mixing well to bind all the ingredients.

Lay out a cabbage leaf and spread a tablespoonful of meat on top. Roll the leaf up and form small parcels (close with a toothpick if necessary). Roll in flour and egg and fry in hot oil. Place in a casserole dish and put to one side.

For the sauce: finely chop the other onion half, one carrot, garlic and parsley, and fry in olive oil. When they begin to brown, add half a glass of white wine and half a glass of stock. Bring to the boil for a minute and pour over the rolls. Check for salt. Cook for twenty minutes on a low heat.

Strain the sauce and serve hot together with the rolls.

ROLLO DE ENSALADILLA
RUSSIAN SALAD ROLL

Ingredients

- 400 g (13 oz) potatoes
- 150 g (5 oz) carrots
- 4 eggs
- 1 tin tuna
- 1 tin peas
- 8 prawns
- 4 slices cooked ham
- 4 rounds white sliced bread
- Mayonnaise
- Salt

Preparation

Cook the eggs, potatoes and carrots separately, in plenty of salted water. The eggs will need 12 minutes to hardboil. The potatoes and carrots are ready when they can be easily pierced with a larding needle. Drain off the water and allow to cool, then peel the potatoes and carrots, and shell the eggs.

Finely chop the potatoes, carrots and eggs and place in a bowl, together with the tuna, in flakes, a tin of well-drained peas and plenty of mayonnaise. Stir well to make sure all the ingredients are mixed together.

Cook the prawns for a minute or two in salted boiling water, then place in cold water before peeling and removing the heads.

Place a tablespoonful or two of the salad on each slice of ham, roll up and place each one on half a slice of bread.

Serve the rolls with mayonnaise, a prawn and grated hardboiled egg.

SALMOREJO
TOMATO AND GARLIC DIP

Ingredients

- 1 kg (2 lb) ripe tomatoes
- 1 kg (2 lb) stale bread
- 2 cloves garlic
- Olive oil
- Vinegar
- Salt

To garnish:
- Hardboiled eggs
- Cured ham
  (*jamón serrano*)

Preparation

Peel and chop the tomatoes. Slice the bread (best if stale). Peel the garlic and cut into two or three pieces.

Place all this in a large bowl and mix with a hand blender. When the ingredients begin to mix together, add a glass of oil bit by bit (in three or four lots), blending constantly.

When the mix is even, add three or four tablespoonfuls of vinegar, salt to taste, and continue blending to form a smooth cream.

Check for oil, vinegar and salt, if necessary.

Place in the fridge to serve chilled, though it should not be too cold.

Serve with a garnish of hardboiled egg and *jamón serrano*.

TARTALETAS DE CENTOLLO Y GAMBAS
SPIDER CRAB AND PRAWN TARTLETS

Ingredients

- 1 spider crab
- 300 g (10 oz) prawns
- 1 lettuce heart
- 1 hardboiled egg
- Puff pastry tartlet cases
- Salt

For the mayonnaise:
- 2 eggs
- Vinegar or lemon
- Olive oil
- Salt

Preparation

Place the crab still alive in a pan with cold water and a handful of salt. Cook for 20 minutes, counting from when the water begins to boil.

Cook the prawns for a minute or two in boiling salted water. Remove from the pan and place in cold water before peeling them and removing the heads.

Open the crab and extract the flesh from the body and the legs, checking for any bits of shell.

Prepare a mayonnaise: in the jug of a hand blender place one egg, the juice of half a lemon or vinegar, and a pinch of salt. Begin to pour in the oil and mix with the blender, using vertical movements, until the sauce is thick enough.

In a bowl, mix the mayonnaise with the crab meat, prawns, hardboiled egg and lettuce hearts, all finely chopped.

Serve spooned into the tartlet cases.

TARTALETAS DE PUERROS Y BACON
LEEK AND BACON TARTLETS

Ingredients

- 3 leeks
- Onion
- 150 g (5 oz) bacon
- 4 eggs
- Puff pastry tartlet cases
- Olive oil
- Salt

Preparation

Rinse the leeks well, making sure there is no dirt between the leaves. Chop finely in julienne, together with half an onion.

Dice the bacon and sauté in very little oil for a minute or so, then remove onto a plate.

Use the same oil to poach the leek and onion on a very low heat, until cooked through but without browning.

Beat the eggs as for an omelette, season and add the vegetables and bacon. Mix well.

Fill the tartlet cases with this mixture and place in the oven to grill until the egg sets.

INDEX

VEGETABLES AND MUSHROOMS

EGGS

MEAT AND POULTRY

FISH AND SEAFOOD

VARIOUS

© EDARA EDICIONES, S.L.
CÓRDOBA - Spain

I.S.B.N.: 84-95332-08-6
Depósito Legal: CO. 195-01

Fourth edition, February 2003

Printed in Spain

Photography
Kike Llamas and Marcos Morilla Studio

Stylist
Natalia Lozano

Translation
Babel - Martin Phillips

Paper
«CreatorStar» by Torraspapel, S.A.